# Writing and Communicating
# for
# Criminal Justice

**WADSWORTH**
CENGAGE Learning™

Australia • Brazil • Japan • Korea • Mexico • Singapore • Spain • United Kingdom • United States

# WADSWORTH
## CENGAGE Learning™

**Writing and Communicating for Criminal Justice**

This supplement has been provided to you free of charge through the generosity of the authors who graciously allowed us to reprint selections from the works below.

Robert E. Grubb, Jr., and K. Virginia Hemby **Effective Communication for Criminal Justice Professionals** © 2003 Wadsworth, Cengage Learning, ISBN 0534149936

Judy H. Schmidt and Michael K. Hooper **6 Steps to Effective Writing in Criminal Justice** © 2003 Wadsworth, Cengage Learning, ISBN 0534172911

Christina DeJong and Daniel K. Kurland **The Internet Guide for Criminal Justice,** Second Edition © 2003 Wadsworth, Cengage Learning, ISBN 0534572634

Lenore T. Szuchman **Writing with Style: APA Style Made Easy,** Third Edition © 2005 Wadsworth, Cengage Learning, ISBN 053463432X

J. Scott Harr and Kären M. Hess **Careers in Criminal Justice and Related Fields: From Internship to Promotion,** Fifth Edition © 2006 Wadsworth, Cengage Learning, ISBN 0534626203

Lance A. Parr **Report Writing Essentials** © 2000 Copperhouse Publishing Company, ISBN 0942728998

Wayne W. Bennett and Kären M. Hess **Criminal Investigation,** Eighth Edition © 2006 Wadsworth, Cengage Learning, ISBN 0534093408

Steven V. Gilbert **Interviewing and Interrogation: The Discovery of Truth** © 2004 Wadsworth, Cengage Learning, ISBN 0534197035

For product information and technology assistance, contact us at **Cengage Learning Customer & Sales Support, 1-800-354-9706**

For permission to use material from this text or product, submit all requests online at **www.cengage.com/permissions** Further permissions questions can be emailed to **permissionrequest@cengage.com**

ISBN-13: 978-0-495-00041-9

ISBN-10: 0-495-00041-8

**Wadsworth**
10 Davis Drive
Belmont, CA 94002-3098
USA

Cengage Learning is a leading provider of customized learning solutions with office locations around the globe, including Singapore, the United Kingdom, Australia, Mexico, Brazil, and Japan. Locate your local office at: **international.cengage.com/region**

Cengage Learning products are represented in Canada by Nelson Education, Ltd.

To learn more about Wadsworth, visit **www.cengage.com/wadsworth**

Purchase any of our products at your local college store or at our preferred online store **www.ichapters.com**

Printed in Canada
5 6 7 8 9 10 11 10 09

# TABLE OF CONTENTS

# PART I

## COMMUNICATION ESSENTIALS

# CHAPTER ONE

# GRAMMAR: A LESSON
# IN THE BASICS

Incident reports are one type of written communication investigating officers are required to prepare. Just as details of the incident must be accurate, so too must the words used to describe the situation. Consider the following example of a robbery incident report:

"I, Officer Jackson, arrived at the location of West 47th and 17th Streets at 05:30. And apon my arrival I spoke to the victim a Mr. Mike Parks. I asked Mr. Parks what had happened and Mr. Parks stated that he was walking home from work, when he crossed the alley way between Little's Bookstore and Dr. Greens florist a noise startled Mr. Parks so he turned to see what the noise was and at that momement Mr. Parks states that a man with a gun pulled Mr. Parks into the alley way and toled Mr. Parks to give him all of his money and watch. The man then pistol wiped Mr.Parks. After taking his statement I called in the detectives and waited for their arrivel. I cleared the scene upon their arrivel."

After reading this excerpt from an actual incident report, do you know what took place? Between the misspelled words and the run-on sentences, this incident report makes virtually no sense. Imagine the impression your department would create if this document were to be introduced as evidence into a court of law. Imagine if you were Officer Jackson; how would you feel if your superior officer asked you to explain your report since he or she could not understand it?

A review of grammar and the role that it plays in written and spoken communication is essential to this text. Criminal justice professionals must be able to write clearly and coherently. Excerpts from reports are often introduced into court proceedings, and superiors review them as part of the investigative process. While entire books have been devoted to the subject of grammar, this chapter will merely review some of the most important aspects of grammar as well as introduce some commonly misused words in the English language. Criminal justice professionals frequently prepare reports, memoranda, and other intra- and inter-departmental documentation. These documents may be reviewed by judges, attorneys, the mayor, and other city officials who form their impressions of you and your organization or department from this writing sample. Therefore, it is imperative that you make the best impression possible by ensuring that your writing sample is grammatically sound and free from error.

**Parts of Speech**

The eight traditional parts of speech are nouns, adjectives, adverbs, pronouns, conjunctions, prepositions, verbs, and interjections.

Nouns. A **noun** is typically referred to as a person, place, thing, or idea. Most nouns are **common** nouns. They name any one of a class or kind of people, places, or things. A **proper** noun is the official name of a particular person, place, or thing and should always begin with a capital letter. Proper nouns include personal names, names of nationalities and religions, geographic names, names of holidays, and names of time units (i.e., months, days of the week).

| Proper Nouns | Common Nouns |
|---|---|
| We'll go to the mall **Saturday**. | What **day** would you like to go? |
| I was born in **March**. | This **city** is beautiful! |
| My horse is in **Mexico**. | What is your **religion**? |

Nouns are also categorized as **concrete** or **abstract**. Because the things they name are physical, tangible, and visible, they are **concrete nouns**. On the other hand, **abstract nouns** name a mental quality or concept, something

4

that exists only in our minds. A review of the following list reveals that many criminal justice concepts fall into the category of abstract nouns.

| Concrete Nouns | Abstract Nouns |
|---|---|
| Book | Truth |
| Plant | Justice |
| Court | Mankind |
| Sentence | Idea |
| Magazine | Love |

Up to this point, we have examined nouns in their singular forms. Another example is a noun used to describe a group of people or things that is considered a single unit. This unit is referred to as a **collective noun**. Some examples of collective nouns follow:

| | | |
|---|---|---|
| orchestra | family | band |
| herd | flock | chorus |
| gang | Congress | audience |
| team | majority | bunch |
| group | personnel | crowd |

The difficulty with collective nouns is in deciding what form of the verb to use with them in a sentence. Is the collective noun singular or is it plural? The answer depends on the meaning of the sentence and where the emphasis is placed. For example, if you are referring to individual members of the group, the plural verb is required. If you are focusing on the group in its entirety, the singular verb is used.

**Singular:** The **chorus** meets at noon every day.
**Plural:** The **chorus** are unable to work together.
Collective nouns also can be used in the plural form—i.e., orchestras, teams, audiences, etc.—when you are referring to more than one group.
In fact, most nouns can be either singular or plural. The greatest majority of them will form their plural by adding an "s" to the end of the word.

| Singular | Plural |
|---|---|
| Desk | Desks |
| Boy | Boys |
| Letter | Letters |

| Report | Reports |
| Book   | Books   |

However, four exceptions to this rule for forming plural nouns exist.

1. **If the word ends in "y" and is preceded by a consonant,**
   change the "y" to "i" and add "es."

   | Forty    | Forties    |
   | Country  | Countries  |
   | Lady     | Ladies     |
   | Category | Categories |
   | Baby     | Babies     |

2. **If the last sound in the word is "s," "z," "ch," "sh," or "x,"**
   then "es" is added to form the plural so that the word is easier to pronounce.

   | Class | Classes |
   | Fish  | Fishes  |
   | Kiss  | Kisses  |
   | Match | Matches |

3. **If the "ch" ending to a word is pronounced "k,"** only "s" is added.

   | Stomach | Stomachs |
   | Monarch | Monarchs |

4. **If a one-syllable word ends in "f" or "fe,"**
   then form the plural by changing the "f" or "fe" to "ves."

   | Half | Halves |
   | Wife | Wives  |
   | Life | Lives  |
   | Leaf | Leaves |

Of course, there are always exceptions to the rule. In this case, **chief and roof** form their plurals by simply adding "s" to the end.

Pronouns. **Pronouns** are used to refer to people, places, or things that have already been mentioned in the sentence. They usually replace some noun. The noun for which the pronoun stands (or replaces) is called an **antecedent**. The antecedent usually comes before the pronoun in the sentence or paragraph. The pronoun and its antecedent must agree in number, gender, and person. That means if you have a plural noun (antecedent), then your pronoun should also be plural. Further, if you have a feminine noun, your pronoun must also be feminine in gender.

I heard **one dog** barking **his** loudest.
I heard **three dogs** barking **their** loudest.
The **man** raised **his** hand to ask a question.
The **men** raised **their** hands to ask questions.
The **woman** read **her** magazine.
The **women** read **their** magazines.

About 50 pronouns exist in the English language. In fact, of the 25 most frequently used words, 10 of them are pronouns. Pronouns are traditionally divided into 6 groups or categories: **personal** pronouns, **relative** pronouns, **interrogative** pronouns, **demonstrative** pronouns, **indefinite** pronouns, and **reflexive** pronouns. In addition to its name, each category has its own definition and special function.

The group of pronouns most frequently used are the personal pronouns. Because of their many forms, however, this group can be troublesome.

| PRONOUNS | | | | | |
|----------|--------|---------|--------|------------|------------------------|
| **Number** | **Person** | **Subject** | **Object** | **Possessive** | **Possessive Adjective** |
| Singular | First | I | me | mine | my |
| | Second | you | you | yours | your |
| | Third (masculine) | he | him | his | his |
| | Third (feminine) | she | her | hers | hers |
| | Third (Neutral) | it | it | | its* |
| Plural | First | we | us | ours | our |
| | Second | you | you | yours | your |
| | Third | they | them | theirs | their |

*<u>ITS</u>: **Often confused with it's (it is).**

7

Relative pronouns often assume the role of the subject of a sentence. More often, though, they refer to nouns that have preceded them. Relative pronouns are **who (for persons), whom (for persons), whose (for persons), that (for persons and things),** and **which (for things).**

Mr. Smith, **whom** I know well, came by my office yesterday.
The boy **who** lived down the street was injured in an accident today.
The car, **which** was red, was his favorite.

Interrogative and demonstrative pronouns are easy to recognize. Interrogative pronouns are **who, what, which, whom, whose, whoever, whichever,** and **whatever.**

**Who** is on the phone?
**What** do you need me to bring to dinner?
**Which** kind of soft drink do you prefer?
**Whom** did you stay with last night?
**Whatever** you mean by "star-crossed lovers," I don't know.

Demonstrative pronouns are used to point to something or someone clearly expressed or implied: **this, that, these,** and **those**.

**That** is the car I want.
**These** are the shoes I've been looking for.
Give **this** to my sister for me, please.

Indefinite pronouns acquired their name because the noun for which they are standing in is indefinite: **everybody, somebody, anybody, nobody, everyone, someone, anyone, no one.**

**Everybody** joined in the race.
**No one** took more time than he did.
Is **anyone** home?

Reflexive pronouns are those pronouns that end in "self" or "selves:" **myself, yourself, yourselves, himself, herself, itself, ourselves,** and **themselves.** The main purpose of reflexive pronouns is to reflect back on the subject of a sentence.

She cut **herself** with the knife. (*herself refers to "she"*)
I bought **myself** a new car this week. (*myself refers to "I"*)
You are just not **yourself** today, are you? (*yourself refers to "you"*)
Reflexive pronouns may also serve to provide emphasis in a sentence. When they serve this purpose, they appear at the end of the sentence.

I will go to the store **myself**.
I suppose I will have to write the paper **myself**.

**Errors To Avoid with Reflexive Pronouns**

You should avoid using reflexive pronouns when your sentence calls for a personal pronoun such as "I," "me," or "you." Remember that a reflexive pronoun should "reflect back" on the subject of the sentence.

NO:     Both Officer Smith and **myself** plan to go.
YES:    Both Officer Smith and **I** plan to go.
NO:     Either Captain Jones or **yourself** will prepare the report.
YES:    Either Captain Jones or **you** will prepare the report.

Verbs. Every sentence **must have** a verb. Verbs express action or a state or being. Verbs can be either singular or plural, depending on the subject of the sentence. Verbs and subjects are like the black and white keys on a piano keyboard; they complement or support each other in the harmony of the sentence. Verbs change tense (time) to tell us when the action is occurring or when the action has occurred as well as what action is occurring. The two main forms of any verb are the present and past tense. The past tense is usually formed by adding "ed" to the end of the basic verb.

| **PRESENT** | **PAST** |
| --- | --- |
| achieve | achieved |
| administer | administered |
| apply | applied |
| approve | approved |
| arrange | arranged |
| assist | assisted |
| brandish | brandished |
| complete | completed |
| conduct | conducted |

| PRESENT | PAST |
|---|---|
| consult | consulted |
| control | controlled |
| coordinate | coordinated |
| decide | decided |
| design | designed |
| develop | developed |
| enter | entered |
| establish | established |
| evaluate | evaluated |
| examine | examined |
| guide | guided |
| help | helped |
| hire | hired |
| identify | identified |
| inspect | inspected |
| investigate | investigated |
| manage | managed |
| monitor | monitored |
| operate | operated |
| organize | organized |
| plan | planned |
| produce | produced |
| provide | provided |
| punch | punched |
| research | researched |
| schedule | scheduled |
| select | selected |
| serve | served |
| shout | shouted |
| slap | slapped |
| solve | solved |
| stab | stabbed |
| supervise | supervised |
| talk | talked |
| train | trained |

As with almost everything in grammar, exceptions always follow rules. While most verbs, called **regular** verbs, follow the foregoing pattern of present and past tense, about 100 commonly used verbs **do not**. Verbs that do not form their past tense by adding "ed" are called **irregular** verbs.

| **PRESENT** | **PAST** |
|---|---|
| am | was |
| cut | cut |
| shot | shot |
| flee | fled |
| run | ran |
| drive | drove |
| drink | drank |
| fight | fought |
| break | broke |
| hit | hit |
| spit | spat |
| dive | dove |
| lead | led |
| know | knew |
| leave | left |
| get | got |
| blow | blew |
| go | went |
| draw | drew |
| read | read |
| lie (to rest) | lay |
| lay (to place) | laid |
| swear | swore |
| write | wrote |
| lead | led |
| build | built |
| teach | taught |

**Errors to Avoid with Verbs**

1.      Learn the irregular verbs. Do not add "ed" to irregular verbs.

NO:     He **hitted** the car with his fist.
YES:    He **hit** the car with his fist.

NO:     I **sweared** to tell the truth.
YES:    I **swore** to tell the truth.

2.      Do not use the present tense of the verb for the past tense.

NO:     Yesterday, he **sees** her twice.
YES:    Yesterday, he **saw** her twice.
NO:     Tuesday, I **says** to my friend, "Let's go to the
        store."
YES:    Tuesday, I **said** to my friend, "Let's go to the store."

3.      Do not shift tenses in the same phrase, sentence, or paragraph.

NO:     He **runs** into the room and **pointed** the gun.
YES:    He **runs** into the room and **points** the gun.
NO:     The officer **forgot** the evidence and **runs** back for it.
YES:    The officer **forgot** the evidence and **ran** back for it.

4.      Make sure that the subject and verb of the sentence agree in
        number (i.e., either both are singular or both are plural).

NO:     All the officers, including Captain Shields,
            **hopes** the criminal is arrested.
YES:    All the officers, including Captain Shields,
            **hope** the criminal is arrested.
NO:     Every one of you **know** your Miranda warning.
YES:    Every one of you **knows** your Miranda warning.

Adjectives and Adverbs. Adjectives and adverbs are modifiers. They always
appear in relation to some other word. An **adjective** modifies or describes a
noun, pronoun, or any other word or group of words playing the part of a
noun. Adjectives tell what kind of, which, or how many.

Living **well** is **the best** revenge.
**The opposing** team played **an aggressive, sophisticated** game.

**Adverbs** modify verbs, adjectives, or other adverbs. They tell how, when, and where.

**Slowly** he turned and saw her waiting **patiently there**.
The book is **more easily** understood if you read **quickly** through the **least** difficult chapters **first**.

Most adverbs end in "ly" but not all do. To add confusion to the situation, some **adjectives** end in "ly" also.

| ADJECTIVES | ADVERBS |
| --- | --- |
| truthful | truthfully |
| intentional | intentionally |
| theoretical | theoretically |
| coward | cowardly |
| hourly | hourly |
| lovely | now |
| lively | quite |
| homely | soon |
| orderly | very |
| friendly | often |
| kindly | then |
| timely | when |
| lonely | down |
| jolly | yet |
| still | |
| here | |
| too | |
| around | |
| almost | |

Rather than the way the word ends, the difference between adjectives and adverbs actually depends on the way the word functions in the sentence. If the word modifies or describes a noun, it is an **adjective**. If it modifies an adjective, adverb, or verb, it is an **adverb**.

Prepositions. Prepositions are connecting words which connect the word or words that follow them to the other part of the sentence. The preposition and the word or group of words that follows it are called a **prepositional phrase**.

## Simple Prepositions

| | |
|---|---|
| **at** the office | **by** the seashore |
| **down** south | **on** the desk |
| **through** the door | **about** the house |
| **for** your love | **like** her sister |
| **over** the top | **beside** the bed |
| **except** you | **across** town |

**Errors to Avoid in Prepositions**

Do not overuse or omit necessary prepositions in formal writing. Remember that by the nature of their definitions, the words we "tack" prepositions to in overuse situations already mean what we are attempting to say. An example of overuse which occurs quite frequently involves "stand up." The word "stand" means to bring your body to an upright position; therefore, to tack "up" to this phrase is not necessary and redundant.

In the other extreme, the omission of necessary prepositions makes your writing nonparallel. Parallelism is an important quality in clear and coherent writing. When you omit prepositions, you allow your reader to interpret the writing; and his or her interpretations may not agree with your original meaning.

Overuse
NO:     Let's divide **up** the paperwork.
YES:    Let's divide the paperwork.
NO:     When did they finally get **down** to the problem?
YES:    When did they finally get to the problem?

Omission
NO:     She was concerned **about** George and his many
        cats.
YES:    She was concerned **about** George and **about** his
        many cats.

14

| NO: | **At** his office and home, he tried to be the same person. |
|---|---|
| YES: | **At** his office and **at** home, he tried to be the same person. |

Conjunctions. Conjunctions are also connecting words, much like prepositions. They connect words, phrases, and clauses. There are four kinds of conjunctions: **coordinating conjunctions, conjunctive adverbs, correlative conjunctions, and subordinating conjunctions**.

Coordinating conjunctions connect parts of a sentence that are equal. The following are commonly used coordinating conjunctions: **and, but, yet, for, or, nor, both, moreover, whereas**. Coordinating conjunctions may join a word to another word: Mom **and** Dad, Jill **or** Mary, firm **yet** kind, slowly **but** surely. They may also join a phrase to another phrase: out of sight **and** out of mind, running down the street **or** meandering through the traffic.

Conjunctive adverbs are used to connect independent clauses and to illustrate the relationship between these clauses. Clauses joined by a conjunctive adverb must be punctuated by either a semicolon or a period. Conjunctive adverbs often serve as transitional words connecting one paragraph to another. Examples of conjunctive adverbs are **therefore, however, consequently, accordingly, for this reason, for example, on the other hand, furthermore, besides, moreover, still, likewise, in addition, nevertheless, indeed, thus, on the contrary, hence**.

He won the choral competition; **consequently**, he went on to have a successful career.

I would like to visit my parents; **however**, I am extremely busy at work and have no time.

His testimony provided many fine insights. **Moreover**, it was eloquently spoken.

Correlative conjunctions always come in pairs: both—and, either—or, neither—nor, if—then, not only—but also, since—therefore. The parts of the sentence they join <u>must</u> be parallel.

**Either** the captain **or** chief must preside.
**Since** you were late, **therefore** I cannot seat you.
**Neither** your crying **nor** your protesting will change my opinion.

Since the sentence elements you join with correlative conjunctions must be equivalent, avoid the following mistakes:

NO:      Her main interests were **that she succeed and running**.
YES:     Her main interests were **success and running**.
NO:      She loved him dearly **but not his dog**.
YES:     She loved him dearly **but she did not love his dog**.

Unlike coordinating conjunctions which connect parts of the sentence that are equal, subordinating conjunctions are used to connect parts of a sentence that are unequal. Some examples of subordinating conjunctions are **as, since, provided that, in order that, until, how, where, because, although, after, when, if, so that, as though, though, before, while, unless, that**. Typically, subordinating conjunctions introduce descriptive clauses and connect to the main clause.

I'll go with you **provided that** you allow me to drive.
**Because** she did not run quickly, she arrived late.
He will call home **after** his meeting.
**If** you dislike the noise of the city, move to the country.

Having reviewed the parts of speech, we will now examine their placement in the sentence structure.

**Parts of the Sentence**

What is a sentence? A sentence may be as simple as two words: **He ran.** A sentence may also be a group or collection of words which may be complex. In either instance, a sentence is designed to convey a complete thought. It is the basis for communication. Every sentence has two parts: **a subject and a predicate**. The subject is the noun—the person, place, thing, or idea. The predicate is the verb—the action taking place. In order to form a complete sentence, you must have a subject and a verb. In some sentences, however, no apparent subject (noun) is present. In these instances, most often commands, the subject is understood to be "you."

[**You**] Run as fast as you can!
[**You**] Drop the gun!
[**You**] Stop the car!

A sentence should have a certain order or design. This order may follow this sequence:

SUBJECT-VERB-DIRECT OBJECT.
James smokes cigars.
Bill drives cabs.

A more complex design may follow this sequence:

SUBJECT-VERB-INDIRECT OBJECT-DIRECT OBJECT
Bill gave me some flares.
The Captain promised me the promotion.

Sentence Errors. Two of the most common and confusing structural problems are dangling participles and misplaced modifiers. These errors create confusion because the sentence is unclear. The reader is forced to try and determine the writer's intent. This lack of clarity is particularly troublesome in police reports that rely on facts and accuracy. The investigator may not interpret the report in the same manner as it was written by the initial responding officer. Furthermore, this ambiguity may present a clever defense attorney with an avenue of attack in the officer's court presentation.

| | |
|---|---|
| NO: | I saw two stores and a movie theater walking down the street. |
| YES: | Walking down the street, I saw two stores and a movie theater. |
| NO: | He found a black Labrador driving his truck through town. |
| YES: | Driving his truck through town, he found a black Labrador. |
| NO: | The officer saw the airplane pulling into his space. |
| YES: | Pulling into his space, the officer saw the airplane. |
| NO: | He climbed the ladder with a bad leg. |
| YES: | He climbed the ladder even though he had a bad leg. |
| NO: | I saw two boys running down the street with a television. |
| YES: | While I was watching, two boys ran down the street carrying a television. |

Sentence fragments, run-on sentences, and a lack of parallel structure are three other common errors. **Sentence fragments** are incomplete thoughts that occur because either a verb or a noun is missing. Sentence fragments frequently occur as a result of police officers writing like they speak in a conversation. Sentence fragments in conversation are acceptable since both parties are present and understand the context of the discussion. However, when only one part is privileged to the communication, sentence fragments damage the integrity of the writer.

| | |
|---|---|
| NO: | And danced for joy at the news. |
| YES: | She danced for joy at the news. |
| NO: | A tree as old as your father. |
| YES: | The tree is as old as your father. |
| NO: | No one. Not even the chief. |
| YES: | No one, not even the chief, could do it. |

**Run-on sentences** occur as a result of a lack of punctuation or an inability of the writer to organize thoughts appropriately. Run-on sentences are often a result of officers attempting to hurriedly write reports due to an increase in calls for service. Occasionally when officers save the report writing task for the end of the shift, run-on sentences are a natural result of this hurried attempt to complete the job and go home.

| | |
|---|---|
| NO: | You run too fast your side will hurt. |
| YES: | You run too fast, and your side will hurt. |
| OR | |
| | You run too fast; your side will hurt. |
| NO: | It was a beautiful day the sun was shining. |
| YES: | It was a beautiful day because the sun was shining. |
| NO: | The suspect said the gun was fired once I think it was fired more. |
| YES: | The suspect said the gun was fired once, but I think it was fired more. |

In an effort to eliminate run-on sentences or to correct them, many writers will simply insert a comma between the clauses. However, they are simply creating another error—**the comma splice**.

| NO: | Speak softly, someone is listening. |
| YES: | Speak softly; someone is listening. |
| OR | |
| | Speak softly, because someone is listening. |

| NO: | If you know, you must tell us, we will handle the investigation. |
| YES: | If you know, you must tell us. Then we will handle the investigation. |

Like ideas should be expressed in a like manner. **Parallel structure** in sentence writing means that similar elements of a sentence are written in similar form.

| NO: | The suspect shot into the roof, wall, and floor. |
| YES: | The suspect shot into **the roof, the wall, and the floor**. |
| NO: | The drunk driver failed to properly perform the heel-to-toe walk, balance test, and the finger-to-nose test. |
| YES: | The drunk driver failed to properly perform **the heel-to-toe walk, balance test, and finger-to-nose test**. |

As mentioned earlier, punctuation is a way to organize thoughts and express those thoughts clearly to others. Punctuation serves as the ties that bind sentences together. Sentences form the foundation of paragraphs and paragraphs act as columns that support the crest or theme of the story the writer is attempting to relate or convey.

**Punctuation**

For the purposes of this chapter, four basic components of punctuation will be discussed. These components are the **period, the comma, the semicolon, and the colon**. The period is the most powerful form of punctuation. It denotes the end of a complete thought. A **question mark** and an **exclamation point** are also used to end sentences. Question marks follow direct questions; exclamation points end emphatic statements.

Go get my newspaper.
Where will we go next?
Would you prepare that report for me?
Let go of me!
Help!

The **comma** is the most versatile form of punctuation. Commas are used to separate words in a series, in dates, and to set off direct quotations. However, one of the most important aspects of the comma may be to separate sentences with two main ideas (compound sentences). One of the ways to correct run-on sentences is to use the comma. A compound sentence has two subjects and two verbs that are typically joined by a conjunction (and, but, or, yet, for, nor). A comma should precede the conjunction in a compound sentence.

He is supposed to be released from prison tomorrow**, but** who knows if his parole will be approved.
She said she was separated from her husband**, yet** she allowed him to enter her apartment.

The **semicolon**, much like the comma, may be used to connect two main ideas in a sentence; however, unlike the comma, it requires no conjunction. A semicolon may also be used to separate items in a series when commas have been previously used in the same sentence. The use of the semicolon in this situation makes the meaning of the sentence clearer.

It was a dark and stormy night; a shot rang out. Violent crimes rose in October, 15 percent; dropped in November, 10 percent; and in December, dropped 5 percent. This indicates no significant increase in violent crimes during the last quarter.

The **colon** is the least frequently utilized mark of punctuation. Colons most often are used to introduce a series or a list.

Only a few of the officers were at roll call: Sgt. Smith, Officer Jones, Officer Jackson, and Officer Johnson.
Please order the following supplies: 50 index cards, 20 envelopes, and 15 pens.

Colons are also used in place of a comma in the introductory salutation of a business letter.

Dear Sgt. Smith:
Dear Mayor Jones:

Proper punctuation is as crucial to the construction of a sentence as the use of the appropriate words. Unfortunately, not only are mistakes made in the choice of punctuation but also in the proper selection of words.

**Frequently Confused Words**

Mark Twain once said, "The difference between the right word and the almost right word is the difference between lightning and the lightning bug." As evidenced by this quote, selecting the inappropriate word changes the entire meaning of a sentence. In today's litigious society, the importance of word selection can be the difference between a dismissal and a judgment. Prior to the sophistication of the 90s, the 60s sitcom, "All in the Family," supplied a wide list of spoonerisms or malapropisms. Archie Bunker's verbal gaffes served as a platform from which to launch a variety of humorous commentaries concerning race, religion, and ethnicity. Today these culturally insensitive phrases would serve to alienate audiences. In this same light, criminal justice professionals need to be very conscious of the words or phrases they select in their spoken or written communication.

| | |
|---|---|
| flee | flea |
| led | lead |
| its | it's |
| there | their/they're |
| passed | past |
| were | where |
| are | our |
| counsel | council |
| except | accept |
| affect | effect |
| know | now |
| no | know |
| knew | new |
| quiet | quite/quit |

| | |
|---|---|
| than | then |
| to | too/two |
| who's | whose |
| your | you're |
| personnel | personal |
| principal | principle |

## Abbreviations versus Full Words

Many abbreviations in writing are standard. We have used them so frequently that they have become second nature, and the full form of the words almost never appears. In other instances, however, abbreviations should be used in only certain circumstances.

## Titles and Ranks

*Mr., Mrs., and Ms.* should be used when they appear before names.

Mr. John Doe
Mrs. Jane Doe
Ms. Jackie **Doe**

*Jr.* and *Sr.* should be used when they appear as part of a name.
Robert E. Grubb, Jr.

*Dr.* should be used when the title appears before a name.
Dr. Grubb

### Civil and Military Titles
You may abbreviate civil and military titles when they appear before a full name. However, you should not abbreviate them when they appear before a last name **ONLY.**

| | |
|---|---|
| CORRECT: | Cmdr. Jim Terry |
| | Capt. Mark Rhodes |
| | Sgt. Angie Howell |
| | Lt. Dickie Parker |

| CORRECT: | Commander Terry |
| | Captain Rhodes |
| | Sergeant Howell |
| | Lieutenant Parker |

| INCORRECT: | Cmdr. Terry |
| | Capt. Rhodes |
| | Sgt. Howell |
| | Lt. Parker |

You may abbreviate **Reverend** and **Honorable** when they precede a full name and do not follow *the*. You may not, however, abbreviate these titles when they appear before a last name alone or when they follow *the*.

| CORRECT: | Rev. Phillip R. Hemby |
| | Hon. Margaret Phipps-Brown |
| CORRECT: | Reverend Hemby |
| | the Honorable Margaret Phipps-Brown |
| INCORRECT: | Rev. Hemby |
| | the Hon. Phipps-Brown |

Degrees and Certifications

Scholarly degrees (B.A., B.S., M.S., M.Ed., Ph.D.) can be abbreviated. An important point to remember is that no other title should precede a name when a degree follows it.

| CORRECT: | K. Virginia Hemby, Ph.D. |

| INCORRECT: | Dr. K. Virginia Hemby, Ph.D. |

**Time, Days, and Months**

Time designations such as a.m., p.m., EST, or CDT are not frequently utilized in law enforcement reports. Most agencies prefer to use the military designation of time (e.g., 0800, 1300, etc.).

| | |
|---|---|
| CORRECT: | The crime was reported at 8:32 p.m. |
| CORRECT: | The crime was reported at 2032 hours. |
| INCORRECT: | The crime was reported at 8:32 PM. |
| INCORRECT: | The crime was reported at 2032 p.m. |

Names of the days of the week and months of the year should be written in full in formal reports and correspondence. However, in officer's field notes or on field interrogation cards, abbreviations for the days of the week and months of the year are acceptable. A note here, though—not all months of the year have abbreviations (March, April, May, June, July).

<u>Days of the Week</u>
| | |
|---|---|
| *Monday* | Mon. |
| *Tuesday* | Tues. |
| *Wednesday* | Wed. |
| *Thursday* | Thurs. |
| *Friday* | Fri. |
| *Saturday* | Sat. |
| *Sunday* | Sun. |

<u>Months of the Year</u>
| | |
|---|---|
| *January* | Jan. |
| *February* | Feb. |
| *March* | March |
| *April* | April |
| *May* | May |
| *June* | June |
| *July* | July |
| *August* | Aug. |
| *September* | Sept. |
| *October* | Oct. |
| *November* | Nov. |
| *December* | Dec. |

**Acronyms and Familiar Initials**

The full forms of initials are often pronounced as words (or acronyms). The full words are almost never written out: *snqfu, tarfu, fubar, WYSIWYG.* The full forms of familiar initials in the law enforcement field are also rarely spelled out: FBI, DBA, ATF, ED, DUI/DWI, CCW, DL/OL, VIN, PI.

**Address Abbreviations**

In law enforcement, geographical locations are frequently cited. For example, *street, avenue, boulevard, road, building,* and *highway* are often used in both written and oral reports.

| | |
|---|---|
| *Street* | St. |
| *Avenue* | Ave. |
| *Boulevard* | Blvd. |
| *Road* | Rd. |
| *Building* | Bldg. |
| *Highway* | Hwy. |

In addition, compass directions are also a major component in offense reports and radio communications. In written form, when a compass direction precedes a street name, it is part of the name and is not abbreviated: *95 Southeast Hickory Street.* When a compass direction follows a street name, however, it indicates a city's section and is abbreviated: *95 Hickory Street, SE.*

Because the use of periods in abbreviations changes from time to time, always check current practice in an up-to-date dictionary. You will find that some abbreviations contain periods, some have optional periods, and some have none.

**State Abbreviations**

The United States Postal Service has designated two-letter codes for abbreviating the names of states. In all but the most formal writing, you have the option of using these abbreviations.

| | | | |
|---|---|---|---|
| Alabama | AL | Montana | MT |
| Alaska | AK | Nebraska | NE |
| Arizona | AZ | Nevada | NV |
| Arkansas | AR | New Hampshire | NH |
| California | CA | New Jersey | NJ |
| Colorado | CO | New Mexico | NM |
| Connecticut | CT | New York | NY |
| Delaware | DE | North Carolina | NC |
| District of Columbia | DC | North Dakota | ND |
| Florida | FL | Ohio | OH |
| Georgia | GA | Oklahoma | OK |
| Hawaii | HI | Oregon | OR |
| Idaho | ID | Pennsylvania | PA |
| Illinois | IL | Rhode Island | RI |
| Indiana | IN | South Carolina | SC |
| Iowa | IA | South Dakota | SD |
| Kansas | KS | Tennessee | TN |
| Kentucky | KY | Texas | TX |
| Louisiana | LA | Utah | UT |
| Maine | ME | Vermont | VT |
| Maryland | MD | Virginia | VA |
| Massachusetts | MA | Washington | WA |
| Michigan | MI | West Virginia | WV |
| Minnesota | MN | Wisconsin | WI |
| Mississippi | MS | Wyoming | WY |
| Missouri | MO | | |

## Capitalization

Everyone understands that the first letter of the first word in a sentence is capitalized. Additionally, we are aware that rules govern capitalization of proper names and titles. However, the rules for capitalizing proper names and titles are complex. Authorities disagree and conventions change. Add to the mix the fact that a word may be capitalized in one instance but not in another. What you need to know is the solution to capitalization problems can be found in standard up-to-date dictionaries or handbooks. "When in doubt, check it out!"

## Capitalization of First Words

As mentioned in the previous paragraph, you should capitalize the first letter of the first word in a complete sentence.

CORRECT:      Students broke the security of the computer system.

You should also capitalize the first letter of the first word in a quotation that begins a new sentence within a sentence.

CORRECT:      Sergeant Jones asks, "Will all the witnesses be present in court?"

If the quotation does not begin a new sentence, however, the first letter of the first word in the quote is not capitalized.

CORRECT:      Mussolini believed that only war put "the stamp of nobility upon the peoples who have the courage to face it."

## Capitalization of Proper Names and Proper Adjectives

Proper nouns are the specific names of persons, places, or things. You should capitalize these nouns and any adjectives that are derived from them. The following are categories that illustrate the kinds of words considered proper nouns and adjectives.

Names of People and Animals (Real and Fictional)
Roy Rogers, James Bond, King Kong

Place Names (Natural and Artificial)
Australia, Delaware River, Washington Monument, Statue of Liberty, Mars

Organizations (Government. Business. Social)
Fraternal Order of Police, Department of State

Historical Names
Tonkin Resolution, Monroe Doctrine, Custer's Last Stand

Religious Terms
God, He, His, Him [referring to God in a religious context]. Palm Sunday

Names in Education
University of Southern Mississippi, Business and Interpersonal Communication, Graduate Record Examination

Awards. Medals, Prizes
Medal of Honor, Bronze Star, Silver Star, Distinguished Service Cross, Purple Heart

Calendar Terms (Days. Months. Holidays)
Friday, July, Memorial Day, Christmas

Product Names-Trade Names and Specific Names
Nissan Pathfinder, Volkswagen Jetta, Sony Walkman, Maytag washer [The common term of a product's name is usually not capitalized.]

Ethnic Terms-Nationalities. Races, Languages
English, Chinese, Sioux, African-American

Scientific Terms-Classifications (except species) and Chemical Abbreviations
0 (oxygen), Au (gold), Alligator mississippiensis

You also capitalize nicknames or substitutes for proper names.

| Official Name | Nickname |
| --- | --- |
| Mississippi | Magnolia State |
| New York City | The Big Apple |
| Mayor Jones | Mayor |

**Capitalization of Titles of Honor or Rank**

You should always capitalize titles of honor or rank when they precede names—whether the titles are governmental, military, ecclesiastical, royal, or professional. In instances where these titles do not precede names, usually you do not capitalize them.

CAPITAL: In Mississippi, Governor Kirk Fordice served two consecutive terms.

NO CAPITAL: Kirk Fordice of Mississippi served as governor of Mississippi after a public scandal involving a woman purporting to be his mistress.

CAPITAL: In 1863, General William S. Rosecrans fought at Chickamauga.

NO CAPITAL: William S. Rosecrans, a general with the Union army, fought at Chickamauga.

CAPITAL: After a serious accident, Professor Hemby resigned from teaching.

NO CAPITAL: After a serious accident, Dr. Hemby, a professor of Business and Interpersonal Communication, resigned from teaching.

**Capitalization of Academic and Professional Degrees**

Academic and professional degrees should be capitalized only when they appear immediately after a name or when they are abbreviated,

CAPITALS: John Henry, Doctor of Laws, died yesterday.

CAPITALS: John Henry, LL.D., died yesterday.

NO CAPITALS: Skip Grubb earned his doctor of laws degree in 2002.

CAPITALS:       Matt Jackson completed his **B.S.** degree in 2002.

NO CAPITALS:  Matt Jackson completed his bachelor of science degree in 2002.

CAPITALS:       Mark Smith, CPA, handled the bookkeeping for the organization.

NO CAPITALS:  An independent certified public accountant handled the bookkeeping responsibilities for the organization.

**Inappropriate Capitals**

The following should not be capitalized:

- Common nouns, even when they appear in phrases that contain capitals

American history
Dell computer
Heinz ketchup

- Words referring to areas of study, unless they are titles of specific courses

CAPITALS:       Economics 121
NO CAPITALS:  economics
CAPITALS:       Algebra II
NO CAPITALS:  algebra
CAPITALS:       Microbased Computer Literacy
NO CAPITALS:  computer literacy

- Words expressing family relationships—mother, father, aunt, uncle, grandmother, grandfather—unless they precede or substitute for names

CAPITAL:        I learned to ride my bike by watching Uncle Ruben.
NO CAPITAL:   I learned to ride my bike by watching my uncle.

| | |
|---|---|
| CAPITAL: | When he was fifty-two, Grandfather had a heart attack. |
| NO CAPITAL: | When he was fifty-two, my grandfather had a heart attack. |

- The words north, south, southwest, and so on when they refer to compass directions. These words should be capitalized when referring to regions.

| | |
|---|---|
| CAPITAL: | The South is changing its image. |
| NO CAPITAL: | Drive south. |
| CAPITAL: | The first trip I took to the Southwest was very exciting. |
| NO CAPITAL: | My house lies southwest of town. |

**Spelling Errors**

Spelling errors are a common problem in written communication. As law enforcement professionals, you must read any documentation closely and slowly so that your eyes fall on each individual word. We have a tendency to "read into" our written documents. We know what we intended to say and when we breeze through our writing quickly with a minimal scan, we are very sure that our words are correct and are spelled correctly. When others read our written documents, however, they note misspelled words, improper word usage, poor grammar, and incorrect punctuation. A good rule of thumb to incorporate into your writing practice is to read each word of your document backwards, thus, you are reading isolated words and not "ideas" or "what you intended to say."

Another method for detecting misspelled words requires you to be alert to those words that have frequently caused you problems. Some of these words may be *received, occurred* and *commitment.* If you pay attention to those problem words, you can then take special care in spelling them correctly.

One electronic means of detecting misspelled words is found on your computer in your word processing program. Most programs (Word, WordPerfect) offer you an opportunity to "check your spelling" when you complete your writing process. These built-in **spell checkers** will check the spelling of words in an entire document or of just a single word. The computer can check hundreds of words in a short amount of time. Unfortunately, even the best of word processing program spell checkers cannot catch nor correct problems such as confusing words— *affect* for *effect, their* for *there, its* for *it's* - since the words are spelled correctly. The form of the word you chose is incorrect.

**Suggestions for Improving Your Use of a Computer Spell Checker**

✓ Keep a dictionary available to use in checking the definition of terms. Do not rely on the spell checker to tell you the correct spelling of a word. Many times the alternative spellings are not useful.

✓ Create a personal dictionary within your word processing program. Proper names, technical terms you use frequently, and other words that may not be included in the computer dictionary can be added. Make sure the words you add, though, are spelled correctly!

✓ Most spell checkers will not find words that are used in the wrong context. If the words are spelled correctly, the computer checker will ignore them. *I told them the dog was over* **their** *and* **Its** *my belief that time heals all wounds.*

**Summary**

In summary, while most criminal justice professionals (police officers, deputy sheriffs, parole officers, bailiffs, etc.) are not particularly interested in nor overly concerned about grammar and sentence structure, these items are just as vital in the preparation and prosecution of their cases as physical evidence or the confession. Inappropriate grammar or sentence structure may jeopardize the credibility or competence of the officer's investigation or testimony. Judges and attorneys have had the benefit of and experience associated with writing courses in law school. Therefore, they may be particularly sensitive to or aware of errors in grammar and sentence structure. If the same amount of care and concern that went into an investigation is given to the spoken word and written report, the credibility of the officer and the organization will be enhanced immensely.

# CHAPTER TWO

# REVISING AT THE SENTENCE LEVEL

Sometimes after struggling to refine the thinking of their papers, writers are distressed that their drafted sentences look so—well, awkward or juvenile. They think, "The content is complex, so why do my sentences look so poorly written?" The brain is unable to think and craft sentences at the same time. Consequently, we can expect the paper's thinking may be clear and precise, but the actual wording of those ideas in sentences will always need some revision.

**Revision Elements at the Sentence Level**

If you are mentally groaning, thinking this chapter is about to launch into the usual review of sentence mechanics and punctuation, you will be disappointed that is not our direction. Instead, we're going to focus on revision techniques that help streamline writing to make sentences smoother, more precise, and less wordy after we remind you about the importance of sentence structure and punctuation.

**The Two Minute Mechanics Review**

That we are not going to discuss mechanics and punctuation in no way indicates we think they are unimportant. But we know that so many other sources, probably including the textbook you used for Introduction to Composition, do such a thorough job in offering writing mechanics explanations and examples that we could not do the subject justice in so few pages. In case you no longer own that writing manual, many colleges have web sites, usually linked to learning centers, offering similar information for your reference. For example, Purdue University's web site (http://www.purdue.edu) has excellent resources for writers.

Because we would be negligent in not even mentioning standard correction areas to evaluate writing at the sentence level, the following chart lists them for you.

| Correction Areas |
| --- |
| **Sentence Structure**<br>Complete sentences, avoiding fragments and run-ons<br>Parallel construction<br>Variety of sentence structures and sentence length |
| **Writing Conventions**<br>Correct capitalization, punctuation and spelling<br>Correct usage of pronouns, subject-verb agreement<br>Avoidance of commonly mistaken words |

### Ensuring Readability through Revision

While writers want to make certain that sentences are grammatically correct, they are aware that other revisions may be needed to ensure **readability**. This term means the reader's ability to read through a document without having to stop to reread confusing sentences or provide apparent missing links in the development of ideas.

You might be inclined to think it's really not that much of a problem. After all, the writer did all the work, so can't the readers contribute something or use their imaginations? It's not quite that simple. If readers have to try to figure out what is being communicated, several outcomes can occur:

1. The readers' interpretations of the material may differ from the writer's intended meaning.
2. The readers' levels of reading comprehension decline after their eyes stop moving forward, having to go back to reread.
3. The readers may lose interest and stop reading altogether.

To ensure readability, we're going to look at four areas of revision: providing transitions, varying sentence pattern and length, choosing audience-appropriate language, and eliminating unnecessary words.

**Providing Transitions**

Transitions, as you know, provide clues to the reader about the relationships between words and between sentences. By including well-chosen transitional words and phrases, the meaning is made clear, avoiding reader confusion or time to puzzle out the connections.

Categories of transitions exist, conveying different relationships. If your repertoire of transitions only includes, "in addition," "later," and "on the other hand," you will want to consult complete lists for those that convey very specific relationships among material including those that
- link similar ideas or add an idea
- limit or contradict an idea or show contrast
- indicate cause, reason, or result
- indicate time or spatial relationship
- indicate a following example
- indicate a comparison

Notice that the underlined transitions in the following sentences clarify sentence relationships.

John left his car running when he went into the store to pick up his dry cleaning. <u>Consequently,</u> the teenager who had just shoplifted several items from the convenience store jumped into John's car and sped out of the parking lot.

Officer Martin Carr is the new police chief in Chatham. <u>Previously,</u> he had been the deputy chief in Clearstream.

**Varying Sentence Variety and Length**

When we write, we choose from 4 basic <u>sentence patterns,</u> each pattern ideally best suited to carry certain kinds of information. Understanding this correlation helps writers create less awkward sentences and increase reading comprehension.

Listed below are sentence patterns and the kind of information appropriate to each one.

35

1.  Simple sentence-carries little information

The first study showed inconclusive results.

2.  Compound sentence-carries two independent clauses whose
    information is equal in importance

Police recruits are trained in defensive techniques, and they learn COP
techniques to relate to the community in a non-confrontational manner

3.  Complex sentence-carries one idea clearly subordinate to the other

Because the car wouldn't start, John missed the 7:00 am train.

4.  Compound-Complex sentence-carries equal and subordinate ideas

After Professor Smith finished seven years' of research for his book, it
was published, and the College immediately promoted him to
department chairman.

Writers also need to consider sentence length as a factor to ensure readability.
If you are interested in pursuing this concept, you can find formulas that show
you how to calculate readability rating of sentences, paragraphs, or entire
papers.  For our purposes, we will follow a general business guideline,
indicating the average reader can comprehend meanings in sentences
averaging 15 words per sentence. For us, as sentence writers, we will have
some sentences with word counts shorter than 15 words and others of more
than 15 words.

Why not make all sentences 15 words if that is the best length?  Several
answers to this question exist.  First, while you may not consciously be
aware of it, your brain registers repetition in language patterns so that the
reader becomes bored with the repetition.  We could compare this
impression to hearing the same song played endlessly or eating the same
food items at each meal.  We become dulled by the experience.

Secondly, writers must consider the information the sentence will carry as a
determining factor in optimal sentence length.  If we are conveying more
complex information, using less familiar terms or words of several

syllables, the information must be carried in shorter sentences to allow the reader to process the message. When we need to convey dense content, we are wise to break the information into a larger number of sentences rather than one longer sentence because of reading comprehension.

If you doubt what we are saying, consider the last time you needed technical advice to troubleshoot a computer problem and called the help desk. After the attendant used "jewel case," "install drivers," and "IPO address" in the first sentence, you knew you couldn't put all the information together.

**Choosing Audience-Appropriate Language**

It is important to know who our readers will be, allowing us to determine which information will be used, where it will be placed, and, finally, how best to phrase material.

Often our research takes us to information written by authorities in the field, i.e. a medical researcher writing about advances in treatment for non-Hodgkin's lymphoma; an economist writing about Vroom's theory of motivation, a forensic scientist discussing new ways to evaluate trace elements of DNA. In those articles we often have to struggle to define for ourselves the more technical terminology, using dictionaries and cross-referencing from other sources to understand the content.

Our readers are often in a similar position of not understanding what we communicate to them. We can help by providing a means for understanding by offering a definition of terms and ideas, comparing the idea to something already familiar to our readers, or stating it in different terms. For example, our medical researcher above might refer to "adrenalechtomized mice" for a medical audience while non-medical readers would better understand the term as "mice that had adrenal glands removed." Note that both terms carry the same meaning, but each conveys it in audience- appropriate language.

While this seems an obvious example, be aware that all disciplines have their own terms and often create "new" words, often not in the dictionary, generally used only within the academic discipline or profession. We call such specific words or abbreviations **jargon**, and, as writers, we have to be aware that jargon does not carry the same meaning to readers outside the discipline/profession. For example, we might read about "M.O. detection"

37

and "PSIR," terms that in all probability carry little meaning to those outside Criminal Justice fields. Therefore, it becomes even more important that we have identified all readers of our paper to determine when, and if, jargon conveys meaning to our readers.

## Eliminating Unnecessary Words

Ironically, many people mistakenly believe strong academic and professional writing should not be understood by the average reader. They think the overly formal style of complicated sentences and elevated, often artificial, word choice, a sort of "showing off what you know," is necessary to reflect the importance of the content. Of course, the reader then needs to be willing to decode the message into easily understood information.

Fortunately, the newer emphasis on academic and professional writing is to make it accessible to its readers clearly and directly with a cleaner style, each word necessary for meaning. When writers use more words than necessary to convey information clearly and completely, they risk burying the meaning inside an avalanche of words, completely nullifying the original purpose for writing.

Perhaps writers should imagine they are charged twenty-five cents for each word used in the paper. The question they should ask about each sentences is "Did I get my money's worth?" If you look at information developed in the following sections to eliminate unnecessary word use, you should be able to say "Yes!"

## Redundancy

Redundancy is word choice that repeats the same idea. Probably all of us have heard the phrase "revert back," redundant because revert means "to go back," or heard advertisers warn us to order now to qualify for a "free gift," again ignoring the meaning of something given to, not paid for.

For your edification or amusement, can you identify why each of the following is redundant?
> close proximity
> biography of Ted Williams' life
> 12 noon
> 12 midnight

shorter in length
summarize briefly

We can also have redundancies within sentences where we repeat the same idea.

Pennsylvania moved to allow voter registration to drivers when they renewed their licenses. This was designed to encourage <u>unregistered voters who had not voted</u> to become involved in the election process. (Unless voter fraud exists, can't we assume this to be the case?)

**Passive Voice**

Verbs have two voices: active and passive. In active voice, the subject performs the action while in passive voice the subject is acted upon. Passive voice will always increase the number of words used.

The police officer <u>drove</u> the car.  (active voice)        6 words
The car <u>was driven</u> by the police officer.    (passive voice)    8 words

Notice that we have increased the number of words, changed the sentence subject from "police officer" to "car," and diminished the power of the verb to "was driven." Additionally, consistent use of passive voice is a guaranteed cure for insomnia because of the longer, dull sentences it produces. Readers have to be very curious to read through papers where the writer frequently uses passive voice. We offer the following paragraph as evidence.

The motion to approve the requirement that front doors be painted red by the occupants was passed. (passive) This bill had been sponsored by Martha Gladstone, owner of Ye Olde Paint Shoppe, and County Historian.(active) It was proposed last year but was defeated by a 7-3 vote against the provision.(passive)

Not only is the paragraph less interesting, it also leaves out crucial information: who performed the actions. Who approved the motion? Who defeated the proposal last year?

Contrast it with this example in active voice."The Commission on the Professionalization of Corrections Officers (CPCO) decided to continue

39

discussion of increasing...." Here we know precisely who did what because active voice provides that information.

In short, passive voice increases word count and generally dulls sentence meaning. However, there are specific instances when writers consciously choose it.

1. when the actor is unknown or unimportant
   A 911call, reporting a possible homicide, was received at 12:42 am.
2. when identifying the actor would assess blame or liability
   A mistake was made in incorrectly flagging your account as overdrawn.

**Combining Sentences**

At the draft stage, sentences exist that don't carry enough information to warrant "spending" the words in weaker sentences. To eliminate this problem, sentences can be combined to make a stronger sentence or the content can be embedded within another sentence.

Embarrassingly, we have all written sentences like the following, short and choppy with a "Dragnet" feel to them.

John went to the registrar's office. He couldn't schedule classes. There was a problem with his financial aid. (18 words)

Notice the sentences are short and connected only because the <u>reader</u> carries over the information to the next sentence.

But, by combining sentences, we slightly reduce word count and more clearly show the relationship among sentence ideas.

John went to the registrar's office, discovering he couldn't schedule classes because of financial aid problems. (16 words)

In other cases, such as the example below, the writer may first need to look at sentence groups to analyze the sentence relationships before writing. The following sentences still have that disconnected feeling and we get duplication of ideas, "confused" and "didn't make sense" as well as word repetition.

The anthropologist was confused when he looked at the mummy. The death mask on the mummified remains of a laborer didn't make sense. Jeweled death masks were for pharaoh use only. (31 words)

Combined, a possible revision could combine three sentences into one sentence that is fairly long.

When the anthropologist looked at the jeweled death mask, used only for pharaohs, on the mummified remains of a laborer, he was confused. (23 words)

It could also be combined into two sentences, clearly reflecting the relationship.

When the anthropologist looked at the jeweled death mask on the mummified remains of a laborer, he was confused. These masks were used only for pharaohs. (26 words)

# PART II

## *ACADEMIC RESEARCH AND REFERENCES*

# CHAPTER THREE

# USING THE INTERNET FOR CRIMINAL JUSTICE RESEARCH

The Internet can be used to *create* new research. Thousands of statistics and data sources are available on-line for students to download and analyze. Because crime data are frequently available to the public, you can easily access data sources and include relevant statistics in research papers and reports.

## Internet Concerns

The resources of the Internet are indeed enormous and ever expanding. Resources unheard-of only a few years ago are now commonplace. But you must first have some idea of what's out there, and know how to find what you want when you want it.

## Know Your Options

Knowing where to look depends greatly on knowing where you might look. You should be aware of the existence of, and uses of, a number of electronic resources – both in general and in criminal justice, such as:
*   Databases (both public and commercial)
*   Abstract services
*   Specialized on-line library connections
*   Professional Associations
*   State and government agencies
*   Nonprofit organizations
*   Usenet newsgroups and listserver discussion groups
*   Anonymous FTP software archives.

**Know How to Get What You Want**

Knowing what is on the Internet, and where it is, is only half the story. You also have to know how to get where you want to go. You must understand the variety of services and the programs necessary to access those services. To use the services effectively, you should understand how each service organizes and accesses information. That means such things as knowing the addresses of relevant web sites and why you might use one search engine over another.

To use the Internet – and your own time – effectively, you must distinguish between active discovery and idle diversion, between productive research and sheer busywork.

**Authorship, Authenticity, Authoritativeness, and Value**

When you pick up a book or newspaper, you have a certain confidence in the authenticity of the material. Examining a book or professional journal in a library, you are aware that it has been selected from among competing texts and reviewed by an editor prior to publication, and selected from among competing publications by a librarian for inclusion in the collection. The title and copyright page attest to the true author and place and date of publication. And you are reasonably certain the document exists in the form intended by the author.

With the Internet, all of these assumptions may fall under suspicion. When it is easy to create personae, it is hard to verify credentials. Internet citations have no page numbers of publication dates, and a reader pursuing a citation may find the text has been moved or altered – with no way to know the difference.

Any source found on the Internet must be judged as to its value and authenticity. These days, anyone can create a web page – your task as a consumer of information is to weigh every source carefully. For example, if you find an article discussing the current statistics on handgun ownership on the web page of the Bureau of Alcohol, Tobacco and Firearms (http://www.atf.treas.gov/) you'll probably think that information is correct. However, if you find different statistics on "Bob's Gun Page", you might question those statistics. Who's Bob? Why does he have a web page about guns? What are his sources? You get the idea – the source of each piece of information should be carefully evaluated before you base your research on it.

On the whole, Internet data is no more authoritative than any other – and in many cases less so. While we may delight in the fact that we can post anything we want on the Internet, when we are looking for information we would like to be able to distinguish beforehand between a professor's treatise and Johnny's seventh grade school report. "Anyone who has attempted to obtain information from the Internet," an editorial in the Journal of Chemical Education observed, "knows that you are as likely to find garbage as you are to find quality information." The affiliation of a server may suggest a certain degree of reliability, but that in itself should indicate neither approval nor review by anyone else at that institution.

While the Internet may have the richness and range of a world-class encyclopedia, that does not mean you want to (or need to) read every article. Much of the current material on the Internet is out-dated or only offers snippets of information. Much of the discussion on newsgroups is simply chatter. Just because you can download thousands of files does not mean you need any of them.

On the bright side, since it is easier to publish material on the Internet than it is to publish books, information available on the Internet is often more up-to-date than information in printed texts. But that is useful only for information that changes frequently, or has changed recently.

### Internet Tactics and Strategies

**Is the Internet the Best Tool to Use?**

You may turn to the Internet to save time, to save effort, or to find better sources of information. But just because you have access to the Internet does not mean the Internet is necessarily the best tool for a particular project. Many times, other procedures are quicker, easier, and more certain to yield results.

**Try the Obvious First**

The general rule should be: Try the obvious first. This seems self evident, but it often needs restating. To find the Latin name for "lions" you can turn on your computer, logon to your Internet service, access a search program, input a search term, wait for a response, evaluate the sources provided, and continue onto a specific location. Or you can flip open a collegiate dictionary and look it up. There's a lesson there.

## Networking for Knowledge

The car manufacturer Packard long ago had a slogan: Ask the man who owns one. With research: ask someone who knows. You can use e-mail to communicate with others, or check archives of frequently asked questions of a relevant newsgroup. You can participate in the communication of a discussion group.

Overall, however, you are more likely to gain fresh insights and understanding through the interchange of talking to someone else than you are punching keys on a keyboard and staring at a computer screen.

## What You Can, and Cannot, Find

The Internet was developed for scientists to exchange data and ideas. While much of the emphasis has shifted to commercial and entertainment application, the Internet remains a vital link in academic and scientific communication.

In recent years governmental agencies at all levels have made increasing amounts of information available on the Internet. Many professional associations and interest groups maintain home pages on the World Wide Web.

Still, no one gives anything of value away for free. While you can access some encyclopedias on the Internet, the premier volume, Encyclopedia Britannica, is available only by commercial subscription.

Full texts of professional journals, are, for the most part, available only to subscribers. Nevertheless, journals increasingly offer tables of contents, archives or abstracts, and supplemental tables, illustrations, or data, as well as searchable indices of past issues on the Internet.

Commercial full-text databases such as Lexis-Nexis can often be accessed via the Internet for a fee. Students and faculty, however, may have access to such proprietary databases on-line or on CD-ROM in college libraries.

**Budgeting Your Time and On-line Time**

The general rule for efficient use of the Internet is simple: log on, get what you want, and log off. You want to know what you're looking for beforehand and have a plan for accessing it. You want to get the information you seek, and get out. This is especially true when you are incurring hourly expenses imposed by on-line services and Internet providers.

You can save time and money by downloading information for later perusal. Off-line time is cheaper than on-line time, and hard copies are easier to read than text on screens.

Both text and graphical interface programs offer some means of automatically capturing on-screen text during a session. You can save hypertext pages on the World Wide Web in a cache directory for closer examination off-line.

Spend your time on-line evaluating information, not looking up addresses. Keep a list of frequently used web sites in your "Favorites" folder or save them as bookmarks. In your career as a college student, you will find yourself returning to those frequently used sites repeatedly.

**Citations and Plagiarism**

You can save time and effort by downloading documents instead of finding published texts and photocopying them. You can then insert that text directly into your own writing.

While a great convenience, this process has obvious dangers. You can confuse your text with text that you have downloaded, and in so doing commit the crime of plagiarism. And you can lose track of information for proper citations.

To avoid plagiarism, store downloaded text with a special font – such as *italic* or SMALL CAPITAL LETTERS – and change the font only when the material has been property cited within your discussion.

The address of Internet documents is often equivalent to the publication data associated with books. The method in which this material is cited in the reference section of your paper will depend on the style you are using, but you can find many sources of information on this topic on-line. There are also some very good style guidebooks such as the <u>Chicago Manual of Style</u> or the <u>Publication Manual of the American Psychological Association,</u> whose most recent versions include citation of on-line sources.

### Resources for Internet Research

There are essentially two approaches to research on the Internet: browsing and searching. Searching begins with selecting a search program or search engine and a search term or terms. Browsing requires, once again, a choice of where to start browsing.

### Browsing

A good start point for browsing is a search engine that groups web sites by topical areas. For example, if you are interested in earning a Master's degree in criminal justice, a list of programs offering graduate programs is a good place to start. If you tried to find graduate programs in CJ by using a keyword search, you would likely end up with a very large number of sites – many of which would not even be relevant to your needs. Instead, a site that groups web sites into categories is a much better solution. Yahoo! (http://www.yahoo.com) is a good example of a hierarchical search engine.

### Searching

There may be times when a keyword search is more appropriate for your needs. Do you have to find a web site that discusses the process of waiving juveniles to adult courts? Since that topic does not fit neatly into one category, we might try to search for the keywords "waiver" and "juvenile" to see if we get any hits.

Search engines that are hierarchical (i.e., grouped by category) are also keyword search engines. There are too many search engines available to list them all--Yahoo! lists 114 "all-in-one search engines" alone. When you include other types that number increases exponentially. The major engines include Google (http://www.google.com),Yahoo! (http://www.yahoo.com), and Excite (http://www.excite.com). As you become more comfortable with the Internet, you will no doubt find one that you are most comfortable with and use it frequently.

## Downloadable Data

The amount of criminal justice data available on-line is truly extraordinary. Even some interest groups have their own data available for download (as with any source, it is vital to assess the reliability of such data before using it). To illustrate some of what is available for students, we briefly discuss three major sources of criminal justice data: The Sourcebook of Criminal Justice Statistics, The Uniform Crime Reports and The National Archive of Criminal Justice Data.

### The Sourcebook of Criminal Justice Statistics

Maintained by the School of Criminal Justice at the State University of New York at Albany, the Sourcebook is an easy-to-use source of criminal justice data (http://www.albany.edu/sourcebook). Statistics are organized by topic, and are available for multiple years.

You will notice that there are two options available for accessing these data. One is called a "pdf" file, and is a graphic image that must be viewed using the Adobe Acrobat program (you can download a reader for free at the Adobe site, http://www.adobe.com). The other file is a "wk1" file, which is a type of spreadsheet file. This file extension indicates that you can download the data into a spreadsheet program, such as Lotus or Excel. The benefit of downloading the data directly to your computer means that you can use a statistical program (such as SPSS or SAS) to analyze the data yourself.

In years past, the information contained in the Sourcebook was distributed by mail to researches. Each yearly volume was the size of a large telephone book, and many researchers (myself included) had an entire shelf filled with volumes of the Sourcebook.

With the advent of the Internet, the Sourcebook no longer needed to be mailed to subscribers. Now it is easily accessible, and searching for the relevant crime statistics is even easier than the old paper version. In addition, the monetary savings are extraordinary – imagine the costs of mailing several thousand telephone books to criminal justice researchers! Today, the same can be accomplished by sending a single email to a subscriber list notifying them of a new version.

## The Uniform Crime Reports

The Federal Bureau of Investigation publishes crime statistics using data collected from law enforcement agencies around the country. Called the Uniform Crime Reports (http://www.fbi.gov/ucr/ucr.htm), these statistics can be used to make conclusions about crime trends around the country – in fact, whenever you read that the crime rate is increasing, news agencies are probably using UCR data provided to them by the FBI.

## The National Archive of Criminal Justice Data

Perhaps the easiest way to find data on-line is through a data repository, such as the National Archive of Criminal Justice Data, which is available through the Interuniversity Consortium of Political and Social Research at the University of Michigan (http://www.icpsr.umich.edu/NACJD/). At the time of this writing, the NACJD contained over 385 data sets available to students at colleges and Universities who are members of the Consortium.

The data files available in the NACJD represent the most current and comprehensive criminal justice data available to researchers. Each data file in the archive is unformatted, with syntax available to read files into SPSS (The Statistical Program for the Social Sciences) or SAS.

## Creating Your Own Data Source

Most undergraduate students in criminal justice will be able to find data sources easily available for research papers. However, some of you may take on more detailed research projects, such as an honor's thesis, in which you create and analyze your own data. While this may sound like an enormous task, it doesn't have to be. You can create a unique research project with some basic research skills and the Internet.

## Using Existing Web Sources

Yet another benefit of the Internet is the amount of publicly available data. Creating a data source is simply a matter of collecting information and entering it into a computer program for data analysis (such as SPSS or SAS).

Let's say you're interested in creating a database of death penalty legislation for each state. You'll probably want to include variables such as:

- Does the state have the death penalty?
- What is the method of execution for each death penalty state?
- How many people are currently on death row in each state?
- How many women and people of color are currently on death row?

Some of this information may already exist in one form or another. You should probably begin by visiting a death penalty site, such as The Death Penalty Information Center (http://www.deathpenaltyinfo.org/). If that site does not contain all the information you need, you may decide to visit the web pages for individual states. Texas, for example, has a comprehensive page dedicated to their Death Row (http://www.tdcj.state.tx.us/stat/deathrow.htm). Finally, news sites may also be helpful in tracking down statistics and information about offenders

## Content Analysis

Content analysis involves creating a data source from media sources. Our purpose here is to provide you with an overview of this technique, so if you are truly interested in this topic we recommend you find a book detailing the specifics of content analysis.

One common use of content analysis involves measuring violence on television. Researchers may systematically watch television every evening during the "family hour" and count how many instances of violence they witness.

A similar type of study can be extended to the Internet. Parents today are concerned that their children are exposed to sexually explicit material on-line. While many of these sites are unavailable to minors, there are of course exceptions to the rule. In some cases, pornographic sites purposefully include key words on their sites that they know are common search terms. These particular sites may be found by children. To measure this, we might want to run a search for commonplace keywords and count the number of sites returned that contain sexually explicit materials.

Newspapers and books are commonly used for content analysis, and with electronic versions of both available on-line, the task of sorting through documents has become considerably easier. You may want to conduct a study of media accounts of terrorism. A study of international newspaper articles might allow you to compare how different countries view the seriousness of terrorism around the world.

## Summary

There are numerous opportunities for criminal justice research on the Internet. We cannot stress enough that extreme care must be taken when determining the validity of on-line sources. Remember that anyone can make a web page stating anything. Try to corroborate all sources.

In addition to literature sources, data sources are also widely available on-line. Many of these are downloadable directly into statistical software packages that can be used in papers and reports.

Supplementing your papers with statistical support will strengthen your arguments, and hopefully result in a high grade!

# CHAPTER FOUR

# REFERENCES IN APA STYLE

American Psychological Association (APA) style writing is a skill often targeted for study in research methods classes, but psychology and other social science students are usually expected to conform to APA guidelines in all of their written work. Sometimes the transition from first-year composition classes to social science classes leaves students confused because first-year composition classes tend to be taught with emphasis on the Modern Language Association (MLA) style. In these courses students generally learn how to write a paragraph, how to write a five-paragraph essay, how to develop a "thesis statement," and how to write a library research paper in the generic (MLA-based) style. This is a useful start, but it does not enhance students' technical writing as much as professors would like.

Students must often master a technical writing style that often contradicts the very "laws" they have learned in their composition classes. In order to master this new style, students are usually instructed to purchase the *APA Publication Manual* and use it as a reference. However, it is difficult for the student new to the style to use the *Publication Manual* in that way. One reason may be that students have little experience reading material written in APA style at this point in their training.

Students often notice that APA style has a *References* section instead of a *Bibliography*. The difference is important. In your References section, you list the works you have referred to in your paper. A bibliography is usually more extensive than a references list and may contain material you read but did not cite. Your references list should be in one-to-one correspondence with the sources you have mentioned in your paper. It should be accurate; readers may wish to consult some of your sources for their own edification.

It should not contain anything you did not actually have in front of your eyes; secondary sources should be listed when appropriate, rather than primary sources you did not read.

---

? REMINDER BOX ?

Include in the references section only those sources that you cited in your paper and only those you actually consulted.

---

If you read only one chapter of a book, you must list only that chapter. Usually, this occurs in the case of an edited book with chapters by various authors. Sometimes, however, you will consult part of a book written by a single author. In this case, the *Publication Manual* provides specific formats for indicating which chapter and/or pages you consulted.

There are so many types of material that may be consulted that it is not necessary to familiarize yourself with all of them until you need them. In this chapter, you will learn about the three most common types of references that occur in student papers: journal articles, chapters in edited books, and authored books (the same person[s] wrote the whole book). If you have used any of the others, consult the *Publication Manual* for details.

**Word Processing Hints**

- The references section begins on a new page, but it has a heading whose level is equivalent to the other major sections (e.g., Results), so it is typed, centered, at the top of the page. The rest of the manuscript (with the exception of the Abstract) is continuous; that is, no other section begins at the top of a page unless it happens to fall that way.

- Double-space everything on these pages, both within and between references on the list. Each entry should begin with a *hanging indent*. That means the first word is at the left margin and all other lines for that reference are indented 1.2 inches.

- Never type authors' first or middle names. Use only their initials and leave a space between initials.

**Journal Article Reference**

Author(s). (Year). Article title. *Journal Title, volume number,* page numbers.
Here are the rules:

1. Authors, last name followed by initial(s).
   - Use the ampersand (&) before the last author.
   - Place a comma between author names.
   - Place the comma before the ampersand, even if there are only two authors in the list.

2. Year of publication.
   - Place it in parentheses.
   - Follow with a period.

3. Title of the article.
   - Capitalize only the first word in the title and the first word after a colon (even if these are only little words like *the*), when applicable.
   - Follow this with a period.

4. Title of the journal.
   - Capitalize each important word.
   - Italicize the title of the journal.
   - Follow this with a comma.

5. Volume number of the journal.
   - Italicize it.
   - Follow it with another comma.

6. Issue number.
   - Almost never include this. Do so only if each issue of the year starts with page 1. Usually, scholarly journals begin each year with page 1, and each issue begins with the page that follows the last one in the previous issue.
   - If you should have to include this, place it in parentheses after the volume number.
   - Do not italicize it.

7.    Page numbers.
- Include the full range (e.g., use 125-127 rather than 127-7 or 125-27).
- Do not italicize the page numbers.
- Finish up with a period.

*Journal article examples:*

- One author:
  Rogers, M. (1989). My sweater has a zipper. *Children's Television Review, 12,* 120-122.

- With two authors, use an ampersand and comma between them:
  Rogers, M., & Kermit, F. (1994). Not all sweaters have zippers. *Children's Television Review, 14,* 12-30.

- With three authors:
  Rogers, M., McDonald, R., & Kermit, F. (2002). Not all creatures wear sweaters. *Children's Television Review, 17,* 127-130.

- With more than six authors, name the first six, then et al.:
  Rogers, M., McDonald, R., Kermit, F., Bird, B., Mouse, M., Brown, C., et al. (1984). And so on. . .

**Chapter in an Edited Book**

**Chapter author(s). (Year). Chapter title. In Book Author(s) (Ed[s].), *Book title* (page numbers of chapter). Place of publication: Publishing company.**

Here are the rules:

1.    Chapter author(s)' last name(s) followed by initials.
- Same rules as for journal article.
2.    Year of publication.
- Same rules as for journal article.

3. Title of the chapter.
   - Same rules as for journal article.
4. The word *In*.
5. Editor(s)' name(s).
   - Initial(s) then last name? not last name first.
   - Separated by commas and ampersand as for authors, but no comma for only two authors.
6. (Ed.) or (Eds.).
   - Follow with a comma.
7. Title of the book.
   - Italicize it.
   - Capitalize only the first word in the title and the first word after a colon, when applicable.
8. Page numbers of chapter.
   - Use the form pp. xx-xx.
   - In parentheses.
   - Follow with a period.
9. Place of publication.
   - City and state or city and country? unless it is well known. If so, use city only.
   - Use postal abbreviations for state.
   - Follow with a colon.
10. Publishing company.
    - End with a period.

*Chapter in an edited book example:*

Smith, T.J., & Jones, R.N. (1971). Very interesting stuff: Relationship between grades and dental cavities. In J. Lennon & P. McCartney (Eds.), *A big book of interesting stuff* (pp. 22-125). London: British Publishing Co.

**An Authored Book**

**Author(s). (year).** *Title***. City: Publisher.**
This is a book written entirely by the same author(s), rather than with chapters contributed by various people.

> *Authored book example*:

> Smart, I.M. (1995). *Fun with psychology*. Green Hill, IL: Green
> Publishing Co.


**Electronic References**

As with the material described previously, this section will not be an exhaustive guide to these formats. Consult the *Publication Manual* or the following Web site for formats not covered here: http://www.apastyle.org/elecref.html. You can check spelling for words like *online* and *Internet* here: http://www.apastyle.org/spelling.html.

When you want to cite an entire Web site, do what I just did: give the address in the text and put no entry in the references list.

But if there is a document you want to cite, notice that you can find all or most of the same elements you need for print documents. Include the author and date in the text and list the full citation on the references page. After you have included all of the information specified for journal articles, indicate what date you retrieved it from the Web and the Web site. Here is an example for a journal article retrieved from the Web:

> Simpson, B. (1999). Cartooning and counseling. *Journal of Multimedia
> Psychology, 2*, 220-227. Retrieved March 5, 2001 from the World
> Wide Web: http://www.apa.org/journals/simpson.html

(You can insert a line break after a slash, but do not use a hyphen.) It is possible that the document you retrieve is not a journal article, but rather an item written by someone just for posting at the Web site. If that is the case, treat it more like a book when you list it. Here is an example:

Simpson, B. (1999). *Cartooning and psychology*. Hollywood, CA: American Psychological Association. Retrieved March 5, 2001 from the World Wide Web: http://www.apa.org/journals/simpson.html

Be careful with final punctuation. Putting a period at the end of a sentence or reference entry that would come after the URL address can cause an error for someone searching for that site. If there is no period in the address itself, leave it off the sentence, too. (See the last sentence in the first paragraph of this section.)

Capitalization rules for URLs are as follows: Everything up to and including the host name (www.apa.org in the preceding example) is in lowercase. The rest must match exactly what you found on the Web.

## Alphabetizing

Alphabetize according to the last name of the author who is listed first in each source. Keep the following in mind:

- Do not rearrange the order of authorship of any given article or chapter. If the article lists the authors as Smith, R.T., & Jones, A.L., do not list them as Jones, A.L., & Smith, R.T.

- Works by the same author are listed by year of publication, with the earliest first.

- If you have the same author listed first with different coauthors for different articles, arrange them alphabetically within the listing for that author, according to the second author of each entry. List Smith, R.T., & Jones, A.L. before Smith, R.T., & Marks, B.J.

- If an author appears as a single author of one source and the first coauthor of another, list the single-author source first and then the one with the coauthor (following the principle that "nothing" goes before "something"). List Smith, R.T. before Smith, R.T., & Jones, A.L.

## References in the Body of the Manuscript

In the text, your citation would look like either of these: "Smith and Jones (1991) found . . ." or "The finds on altruism (Smith & Jones, 1991) . . . "

The latter is usually preferred. The authors' names are typically not relevant to the point you are making, and if they are not directly relevant, then they are parenthetical.

When you are quoting from a source, use double quotation marks. Single quotation marks are only used when the author you are quoting is quoting someone else. In that case, the source contains double quotation marks, and these become single quotation marks in your manuscript. Final punctuation goes inside the quotation marks. When your quotation contains 40 or more words, use block form. That means that instead of using quotation marks, place the entire quotation in indented form. Indent one-half inch from the left margin (in line with the start of paragraphs) and keep every line of the quotation indented just the same amount. Do not change the right margin; use the same right margin as in the rest of your manuscript.

You will have to cite the page number of the source for direct quotations. Do so after the closing quotation mark and before the period:

Freud (1950) reported "Blah blah blah" (p. 23).

If you want Freud's name in parentheses, do it like this:

"Blah blah blah" (Freud, 1950, p. 23).

When this occurs after a block quote, it comes after the final punctuation:

Mary had a little lamb whose fleece was white as snow.
Everywhere that Mary went the lamb was sure to go. He
followed her to school one day which was against the rule.
The teacher was surprised to see a lamb at school. (p. 23)


Page references for online sources can be challenging; they are not paginated. If paragraphs are numbered, use that number (e.g., para. 3). If they are not, use headings as locations (e.g., Explicit Communication section).

Here are some final quirks for referencing in the body of your paper:

- Use the ampersand in parentheses and the word *and* in the text.

- Use commas only for three or more authors.

- When the work has two authors, always use both names (Michael & Jordan, 1987). When it has more than two and fewer than six authors, name them all the first time you cite them (Reebok, Nike, Keds, & Converse, 1988). In future references, name only the first and use *et al.* instead of the rest of the names on the list. (Reebok et al., 1988). When the work has six or more authors, use et al. after the first author's name even the first time you cite them.

- If you are referring to more than one article inside the same parentheses, use a semicolon to separate the references. List them in the same order as they would appear in the References section. Here is an example: This hypothesis has received robust support (Ames, 1991; Roberts & Emerson, 1993; Simmons et al., 1990).

# PART III

## PROFESSIONAL COMMUNICATION SKILLS

# CHAPTER FIVE

# THE RÉSUMÉ:
# SELLING YOURSELF ON PAPER

*Reprinted with permission from*
**Careers in Criminal Justice and Related Fields:**
**From Internship to Promotion**, Fifth Edition
*by* J. Scott Harr and Kären M. Hess
© 2006 Wadsworth/Thomson Learning

*Writing a Résumé: Spend time on self-assessment first. Identify all the achievements of your past that illustrate skills. Describe them in active verbs and look for consistencies. That's the clue as to what you should emphasize. A résumé is scanned, not read. It's a sales tool that should give someone a sampling, not details in full.*

-Jean Clarkson

Think about your goals and yourself, your fitness, education and attributes. It's time to pull all this information together into one of your most important job-seeking tools—the résumé.

Résumé is a French word (pronounced REZ-oo-may) that means "summary." You probably know what a résumé is, but that's a little like saying you know what surgery is. A vast amount of territory exists between recognizing a concept and grasping its true meaning. To have a working understanding of such a concept is even more involved. This chapter provides you with a working knowledge of the résumé.

## What is a Résumé?

Webster's defines *résumé* as: "A short account of one's career and qualifications prepared typically by an applicant for a position." Résumé guru Yana Parker (http://www.damngood.com) offers a more dynamic definition: "A résumé is a self-promotional document that presents you in

67

the best possible light, for the purpose of getting invited to a job interview. It's *not* an official personnel document. It's not a job application. It's not a 'career obituary'! And it's not a confessional."

And the sales pitch must work quickly. The *Land That Job!* Website (http://www.landjob.com) states: "Your resumes and resume cover letters can be reviewed and rejected in as little as 5 seconds! Both must communicate your qualifications at a glance." According to *Resume.com*: "Most staffing managers and recruiters (headhunters) scan and discard each resume in 10 to 15 seconds unless the resume provides them with a compelling reason to flag it for an in-depth review."

The competition to attract an employer's attention is keen, bitter and brutal. A well-prepared résumé can be the determining factor in whether an employer calls you for an interview, allowing you a "foot in the door." Your résumé may be your first contact with a potential employer. It may also be the last. The choice is yours.

In some cases, however, particularly in larger agencies and institutions, résumés are not used. Instead, the agency goes through a civil service commission. Applicants fill in only the commission's paperwork and can add nothing to it. A résumé can backfire if you include it and it is *not* asked for or wanted.

**The Purposes of the Résumé**

The résumé serves both the employer and prospective employee. The résumé is important to the *employer* because it helps weed out unqualified candidates. For most employers, this is the most important function of a résumé. Employers will use *any* flaw in a résumé to cut down the number of individuals to be interviewed. Résumés help employers cut through a lot of preliminary questioning about applicants' qualifications and help employers structure their interviews.

The résumé is important to *you* because it can help get you in the door for an interview. In fact, Barthel and Goldrick-Jones (http://www.rpi.edu/web/writingcenter/resume.html) assert: "A resume has one purpose: to get you a job interview." JobWeb (http://www.jobweb.com/resumes_interviews/resume_guide/res.htm)

presents the résumé's purpose another way: "A resume does its job successfully if it *does not* exclude you from consideration."

The résumé serves other purposes as well. Preparing your résumé will force you to take a hard look at your skills, qualifications, past experience and accomplishments. It will require you to recall (or look up) dates and addresses. It will compel you to organize your past clearly and concisely, which will help you present yourself in an organized manner during the interview as well. This will enable you to approach the interview confident that you have the qualities and background the employer is looking for, or why would you be called in?

During the interview, the résumé will save time by providing a common ground to start from. It will also keep you honest. The temptation to exaggerate your experience or accomplishments will be removed when you know the employer has seen your résumé. Now that you know how important your résumé is, look at the specific steps in creating one.

**Steps in Creating a Résumé**

Creating a résumé is like painting a picture of yourself. From the conception of the idea to the completion of the masterpiece, you need to take seven specific steps.

The seven steps to creating a résumé are:

1. Compile all relevant information.
2. Select the most appropriate type of résumé.
3. Select a format.
4. Write the first draft.
5. Polish the first draft.
6. Evaluate the résumé and revise if necessary.
7. Print the résumé.

Creating an effective résumé is *hard work*, but the results will be well worth it. Without an effective résumé, you are wasting your time applying for most jobs. You won't get to first base. Even if an agency does not require a résumé, they will expect you to be a "living résumé" at the interview. Get yourself organized before that. Make up your mind to devote several hours to this important document.

**Compile Information**

Gather all the information that could possibly be included in your resume. Some will be used; some won't. Painters gather all of their brushes and paints before they begin to work so they aren't interrupted during the creative process. Likewise, you will want to gather all the information you *might* decide to include. You don't want to interrupt the creative writing flow to look up a phone number or address.

You'll look at three kinds of information: (1) data you must include, (2) data you might include and (3) data you should probably not include but should be prepared to discuss. Don't guess at dates. Verify them. Don't guess at addresses. Check them out if it's been awhile since you worked or lived somewhere.

Look first at what *MUST* be included: personal identifying information, your educational background and your work experience.

**Personal Identifying Information**

**Name.** Obvious? Yes. But believe it or not, some people actually forget to include their name. In addition, think carefully about how you want your name to appear. Do you want to include your middle name? An initial? A nickname? A title? If you include a nickname, put it following your first name with quotation marks around it, like this: *Robert "Bob" T. Jones.* This lets the employer know what you prefer to be called. Avoid extreme or inappropriate nicknames such as "Killer." Parker advises: "Don't mystify the reader about your gender; they'll go nuts until they know whether you're a male or female. So if your name is Lee or Robin or Pat or anything else not clearly male or female, use a Mr. or Ms. prefix."

✓   How do you want your name to appear in your résumé? Write it down.

**Address**. It is usually best to give only your home address. Put the street address on one line. Do not abbreviate. Put a comma between a street address and an apartment number. Put the city and state on the next line and separate them with a comma. Use the two-letter state abbreviation—both letters capitalized and NO period. Include your zip code. Do *not* put a comma between the state and zip code.

|            |                                |
|------------|--------------------------------|
| Example:   | 123 Third Avenue South, #401    |
|            | My Town, MN 55437               |

✓ How should your address appear? Write it down.

✓ If you move frequently, you may want to include a permanent address in addition to your present address.

✓ E-mail address: E-mail is no longer a novelty or luxury—it is how most businesses communicate today. If you don't currently have an e-mail address, we suggest you obtain one because (1) it makes it easier for prospective employers to contact you and (2) to not have one in today's online climate reflects negatively on your technological, specifically computer, skills. Remember to check your e-mail daily.

**Phone number.** *Always* include a phone number. Busy employers often prefer to call rather than write. Make it easy for them. Give the area code, followed by a hyphen and then your phone number. Indicate if it is a home, work or cell number. Many people prefer to *not* include a work phone to avoid being called at work. Would getting job-search related phone calls at work cause you any problems? If so, do *not* include your work number. Some people also include the hours they can be reached at a given number. Others put this information in their cover letter.

|          |            |                                   |
|----------|------------|-----------------------------------|
| Example: | Work Phone | 612-555-9929 (9 am to 5 pm)       |
|          | Home Phone | 612-555-8818 (6 pm to 10 pm)      |
|          | Cell Phone | 612-555-2222 (9 am to 10 pm)      |

Did you know there was so much to think about in simply giving your name, address and phone number?

### Education

Information about your education is crucial to your résumé.

✓ **College.** List each college attended, city and state, number of years completed, major/minor, unique areas of study and degree(s) earned. Start with the most recent and work backward. Include any honors, awards or leadership positions. Include grade point average *if* outstanding.

✓ **Professional Schools.** Include the same information as for colleges. Include academies here also.

✓ **Internships.** Include the place and length of the internship.

✓ **Certificates.** Relevant certificates would include first aid, CPR and the like. Give the year the certificates were awarded and expiration dates, if relevant.

✓ **Other Educational Experiences.** Include any relevant seminars, workshops, correspondence courses and the like.

✓ **High School.** Include name, city and state, year of graduation, and grade point average if it is outstanding. Include your high school *only* if you graduated within the last 10 years or if you have no other education to include.

**Work Experience**

Past general employment of any type is valuable in the job search, even if not related to your field. Volunteer experience, work-related or not, should also be included on your résumé. Of special importance are the qualifications and skills you bring to the job. Your résumé should stress achievements more than education and experience.

✓ Begin with your present job, or your most recent job if you are not currently employed. Work back in time. Use the work experience section to describe your qualities and skills wherever and however you can. If applicable, you might demonstrate these qualities and skills in the education portion of your résumé as well.

Several other areas of information might also be included in your résumé, depending on your background. Even if you decide *not* to include much or most of the following information, it is important for you to think about it and have it clear in your mind because it could come up during the interview.

**Position Desired or Employment Objective**

What specific job do you have in mind? Are you open to *any* position in your chosen field? This information can be very helpful to busy employers as they skim through stacks of résumés. An attractive job candidate is one who knows what he wants to do. In fact, to the question: "What is the most common résumé mistake made by job hunters?" Parker replies: "Leaving out their Job Objective! If you don't show a sense of direction, employers won't be interested. Having a clearly stated goal doesn't have to confine you if it's stated well."

✓ Write down the position desired and, if relevant, your employment objective. An example might be: *Position desired: Entry-level officer with opportunity to provide* _____.

✓ Tell what you can do for the employer—not what the employer can do for you.

**Other Information**

Other information that may be put in your résumé includes the following:

✓ Willingness to travel or relocate, military experience, professional memberships, knowledge of foreign language(s), foreign travel, awards, publications, community service or involvement, interests and hobbies. Also, list your accomplishments and don't be modest.

✓ You might also want to include your availability—can you start immediately or do you need a certain amount of time to give notice to your present employer? Can your present employer be contacted?

**References**

If you get to the point in the hiring process where you are being considered, most employers will want to check your references.

✓ Choose references now and write them down. Try to have business, professional and academic references as well as personal references.

Choose your references carefully. *Always* ask your references if they are willing to provide you with a *positive* reference. Most people do *not* include the references in their résumés. You can simply state: "References available on request," and prepare a separate sheet of references to make available to employers who request them. This also keeps your references confidential until a request is made for them.

## Photograph

Some books on résumés suggest that a photograph should never be included with a résumé; other books highly recommend it. Those who are against it suggest that it violates antidiscrimination laws by providing information an employer cannot legally ask about. For example, race, sex and approximate age are revealed in a photograph. If you feel these factors may work in your favor, you may decide to include a photograph.

One advantage of including a photo is that it will probably make your résumé stand out from the rest, always a primary goal. However, unless it represents you in a way the employer will appreciate, the photo could detract from your résumé. If you do include a photo, be certain it is recent, professional and puts you in a favorable light. You should be neatly groomed, and the reproduction should be clear and crisp.

## What *Not* to Include

What not to include is a matter of opinion. While you will *never* lie on a résumé, you will want to present yourself so that even negative occurrences look good for you. If you have to explain them in depth during an interview, that's fine, as long as you *get* to the interview.

Including too much data is a major fault of many résumés. Not only does this create a document that is so long it won't get read, but you can harm yourself by saying too much. For example, do not state in a résumé why you left past jobs. Newfield (2004) warns: "'Company sold,' 'Boss was an idiot,' and 'Left to make more money' have no place on your résumé." If the reason was somewhat spectacular, for example a series of promotions, put it in, but the presumption will be that you moved upward and onward to better positions. Also, the résumé is not the place to explain difficulties you've had. It is a chance to provide a **brief** overview of yourself, to be expanded on once it has gotten you an interview. Be certain everything you include is relevant and cannot in any way detract.

Exceptionally personal data can also detract from the emphasis that should be on your skills and qualifications. Newfield asserts: "Personal information does not belong on a résumé in the United States. Don't include information on your marital status, age, race, family or hobbies." Parker advises:

> Don't include hobbies on a résumé unless the activity is somehow relevant to your job objective, or clearly reveals a characteristic that supports your job objective. For example, a hobby of Sky Diving (adventure, courage) might seem relevant to some job objectives (Security Guard?) but not to others….

> Don't include ethnic or religious affiliations (inviting pre-interview discrimination) UNLESS you can see that including them will support your job objective. Get an opinion from a respected friend or colleague about when to reveal, and when to conceal, your affiliations.

### Select the Type of Résumé

When you go fishing you select the bait that will best serve your purpose based on the specific conditions at that particular time and the fish you're after. Likewise, you should have all the "bait" you need to land an interview in the form of the data you have just put together. Now decide how to present it. Three basic types of résumés are commonly used:

➢ Historical or chronological

➢ Functional

➢ Analytical

Each type has a specific format, content and purpose.

**Historical/Chronological Résumé**

The historical/chronological résumé is the most traditional and is often considered the most effective. As implied by the name, this style presents information in reverse chronological order, starting with your most recent work experience and moving back in time to your past work experience. Both education and employment lend themselves to this style. Always include dates and explain any gaps in the chronology.

The historical/chronological résumé is easy to read and gives busy employers a familiar form that can be quickly read. It is the best format to use when staying in the same field. It is not the best format if you have little related experience. Use a chronological résumé if:

➤ You have spent three or more years with previous employers and have not changed jobs frequently.

➤ You are seeking a position in the same field in which you have been employed.

➤ You have worked for well-known, prestigious companies.

➤ You can show steady growth in responsibilities.

**Functional Résumé**

The functional résumé stresses experience and abilities as they relate to the job you are applying for rather than a chronological listing of past employment. Dates do not receive as much attention. Hofferber (2004) suggests:

> If you've held a number of different or unrelated jobs during a relatively short period of time and are worried about being labeled as a job-hopper, the functional résumé (also known as a "skills-based format") could be the answer for you. This format can also work well for those entering the workforce for the first time or after a long absence (such as recent grads with no formal work experience, stay-at-home moms or dads now seeking outside employment, or caregivers who have spent a year or more treating an ill or aging family member.) It could

also be a good choice if your prior work experience is more relevant to your current job target than what you're doing presently.

This style emphasizes a candidate's strengths in key skills categories and maximizes scant work experience while minimizing irrelevant jobs, employment gaps and reversals. Use a functional résumé if:

➢ You are seeking a job in a field new to you.

➢ You have been unemployed for more than three months.

➢ Your responsibilities are complicated and require explanation.

➢ You can point to specific accomplishments on your last job.

➢ You are competing with younger applicants.

## Analytical Résumé

The analytical résumé stresses your particular skills. It is especially helpful if you are changing career goals but you have obtained necessary skills and qualifications from your present and past jobs. It lets you stress those *skills* and *talents* instead of your work history. Dates are usually omitted, but past jobs and experiences are referred to at some point. Again, you must determine if this approach can best reflect your particular abilities.

## What about Creativity?

You may be wondering if these three styles are rather boring. You may want to be somewhat more creative. Think carefully about it. An imaginative or creative approach may be of great benefit, or it may burn you. The positive side of such an approach is that it may set your résumé apart from the dozens, hundreds, even thousands of others, thus receiving the attention it deserves. The negative side of a creative résumé is that it might be the reason the employer is looking for to jettison your résumé, along with any others that do not appear "normal." Remember, many employers feel a résumé is a business matter and should be presented in a businesslike manner.

If you decide to use an imaginative/creative résumé, be sure to include all the information any other style would present. If you can do so, you just might be on to something. For example, what could possibly catch a police department's eye quicker than a résumé that takes on the appearance of a "Wanted" poster? It might work, but give very serious consideration to such an idea at an entry-level position.

**Format the Résumé**

The format is the layout of the information—what comes first, second and third. The format should be attractive, businesslike and professional. Actually *design* your format on a sheet of paper. *Block* your material and use *headings* to guide the reader.

Plan for margins at the top, bottom and sides. Use white space freely. Will you center your identifying information? Have it flush left? Will you use one or two columns for the bulk of the information? Try to fit all the information on *one* page. However, if you need two pages, use them. Reducing the font size just to fit everything on one page can become problematic for the employer. Newfield recommends: "If your career warrants a two-page résumé, then go ahead and create a document that reflects the full range of your experience and accomplishments. Don't reduce the type size to such a degree that your résumé becomes difficult to read."

Keep in mind: If your résumé is too long, you risk it not being read; too short, and you risk leaving out relevant information.

*Note*: Formatting considerations for e-mailed résumés and other computer compatibility issues are discussed later in this chapter.

**Write the Résumé**

If possible, use a word processor to write your résumé. This will make editing and updating it less painful and e-mailing it much easier.

The traditional advice for writing an effective résumé has been to use short, action-packed *phrases*.

**Short.** Omit all unnecessary words. This includes:

➤ Personal pronouns: *I, me* and *my*

➤ Articles: *a, an* and *the*

**Action-Packed.** Write with *verbs*, not with *nouns*. For example, don't say *conducted an investigation*, say *investigated*. Writing with verbs is also shorter than writing with nouns. Look at the following:

> I conducted an analysis of all the incoming calls to the dispatcher, and I compiled detailed analytical reports based on my analysis.

*Twenty-two words.* Eliminate the pronouns (*I, my*) and articles (*an, the*) and use verbs instead of nouns. What you'll get is something like the following:

> Analyzed all incoming calls and wrote detailed reports.

Which statement would you rather read? Which conveys an image of the writer as focused and authoritative?

**Phrases.** Phrase your writing. Watch where lines end. Avoid hyphenating words at the end of the line. For example, read the following:

> It was a difficult job because my boss was a rat-
> her rigid person.

Get the idea? Pay attention to effective ads on television and in print. Notice how the words are strung together for maximum effect. You can do the same in your résumé. Try using short "bullet" phrases that begin with active verbs. Strive for variety in your verbs. Here are some that might fit your experience:

| | | | | |
|---|---|---|---|---|
| achieved | consulted | guided | organized | scheduled |
| adapted | controlled | hired | planned | selected |
| administered | coordinated | identified | presented | served |
| analyzed | decided | improved | produced | set up |
| applied | delegated | increased | proved | solved |
| approved | designed | inspected | provided | spoke |

| | | | | |
|---|---|---|---|---|
| arranged | developed | invented | published | supervised |
| assessed | edited | investigated | recorded | surveyed |
| assisted | educated | led | redesigned | taught |
| built | encouraged | managed | represented | trained |
| chaired | established | modified | researched | updated |
| completed | evaluated | monitored | reviewed | wrote |
| conducted | examined | operated | revised | |

Parker suggests:

> Fill your resume with "PAR" statements. PAR stands for
> Problem-Action-Results; in other words, first you state the
> problem that existed in your workplace, then you describe
> what you did about it, and finally you point out the beneficial
> results.

> **Here's an example:** "Transformed a disorganized, inefficient
> warehouse into a smooth-running operation by totally
> redesigning the layout; this saved the company thousands of
> dollars in recovered stock."

> **Another example:** "Improved an engineering company's
> obsolete filing system by developing a simple but
> sophisticated functional-coding system. This saved time and
> money by recovering valuable, previously lost, project
> records."

**Preparing an E-Résumé**

According to Challenger (p. 6): "Computers and the Internet have changed
the way résumés are written, distributed and read...Today, employers use
sophisticated computer programs to scan in-house and independent
databases that can contain tens of thousands of résumés. These programs
search for selected words and phrases that best apply to their ideal
candidate." When creating an e-résumé, the rule about sticking to one page
becomes more flexible because the programs used to scan résumés for
keywords can comb through a two-page résumé just as easily as a single-
page one. And as Challenger (p. 6) warns: "E-resumes that are too short are
less likely to contain the magic phrases."

To prepare an e-résumé to be most compatible with a variety of electronic databases, use a common typeface, like Courier or Arial. Challenger (p. 6) cautions: "Exotic fonts may not be readable by the employer's computer." Keep the font size between 10 and 14 points; and avoid italic and boldface type. Hayes (2000, p. 15) adds: "Instead of avoiding jargon, *use it often—* computers target words specific to and industry and are likely to select resumes containing those words multiple times." Challenger (p. 6) suggests including a keyword section at the end of your résumé with as many variations of applicable words as possible.

As more companies go online, "Please e-mail your résumé in ASCII format," is becoming an increasingly common statement in job listings. ASCII (pronounced "askee") files or text-only documents do not retain special formatting commands, thus allowing different word processing applications to read and display the same text information. Guidelines to follow when creating an ASCII-formatted résumé are:

➢ Do not use special characters such as mathematical symbols.

➢ Use your spacebar rather than tabs.

➢ To indent a character or center a heading, use the spacebar.

➢ Use hard carriage returns to insert line breaks, not the word-wrap feature.

➢ Font size and typeface will be whatever your computer uses as its default, so boldface, italics and various sizes will not appear in the ASCII version.

➢ Always run a spell-check on your document before you save it as text-only file.

➢ Instead of bullets, use asterisks or plus signs at the beginning of lines.

➢ Instead of lines, use a series of dashes to separate sections. Don't try to underline text.

A basic rule of thumb is to keep it simple, as if you were using an ancient typewriter with no function keys or fancy formatting devices.

**Preparing a Scannable Résumé**

It is common practice in many companies to scan résumés received via regular mail so they may easily search for keywords and transmit the document to any and all interested parties. The scanning process uses Optical Character Recognition (OCR) software to convert hardcopy images into digital computer data. Fancy graphics, complicated formatting and general clutter typically do not scan readily, and the résumé that appears on the recruiter's monitor may simply look too messy and unappealing to even warrant a read-through. Isaacs (2004b) offers the following tips for creating a scannable résumé:

> Since companies use different scanning hardware and software, it is impossible to know for sure how to format a resume. The best way to ensure that the document is formatted properly is to call the company's HR department and find out if they have specific guidelines. If you don't have this information, there are steps you can take to optimize scannability:
>
> - One of the most important factors is whether or not letters touch each other. Scanning systems have difficulty interpreting characters that are melded into one, so make sure that no characters touch each other. Italics and bold are both fine, as long as the letters do not touch.
> - Choose a common, nondecorative sans serif font (such as Arial or Optima) and keep the font size between 10 and 14 points.
> - Underlining and horizontal/vertical lines are okay, as long as the lines do not touch any of the letters.
> - Avoid columns (the OCR reads the text from left to right).
> - Do not use round, hollow bullets (they may be interpreted as the letter o). Instead, choose round, solid bullets.
> - Do not use ampersands, percent signs or foreign characters (they may not translate properly).
> - Add a space in between slashes so that the slash doesn't touch the letters (e.g. IT / IS).
> - Use light-colored paper (white is best) and avoid paper that contains dark speckles.
> - Do not staple your resume.

- Mail your resume in a flat envelope. If you fold your resume and the crease lands on a line of text, the laser toner may flake off and render the entire line unreadable.
- Make sure you have keywords throughout your resume, so that you will be found in a database search.

## Tailoring Your Résumé

*A final suggestion*: Tailor your résumé to fit the job. With all the preceding suggestions and choices, you may find it difficult to settle on one "perfect" format or word choice for your résumé, especially if you are applying to a variety of types of employers. So don't. To the common dilemma: "What if I have several different job objectives I'm working on at the same time? Or I haven't narrowed it down yet to just one job target?," Parker advises: "Then write a different resume for each different job target. A targeted resume is MUCH, much stronger than a generic resume."

Once you have written your first draft, let it sit overnight. You will then be ready to edit and polish it.

## Edit and Polish Your First Draft

First drafts simply don't cut it. Continue to work with it until it has the punch you want. Because employers are busy, say as much as you can with as few words as possible. Spend time refining each phrase. Work at developing brief statements that explain clearly and strongly what your education and experience are, what opportunities you've taken advantage of and what qualifications and skills you would bring to the job.

You might consider hiring a professional editor or even a professional résumé writer at this point. Using such services will be less expensive if you have completed all the background research, designed a format and written the first draft. Razek (2001, p. 12) states: "For a fee, Vault.com's career experts evaluate your resume and provide career coaching by phone. Prices range from $39-$319." The web address is: http://www.vault.com/careerservices/careerservices.jsp

*Proofread* your draft. Check the spelling of every word. Check every capital letter and punctuation mark. Then check it again. Better yet, have a friend whose writing skills you respect check it for you. It is very hard to see your own writing errors. Some people find it helpful to proofread by going from right to left in each line, looking at each word. Morem (2001 p. D2) provides the following examples of real résumé gaffes:

➤ "Worked party-time as an office assistant"

➤ "Planned and held up meetings"

➤ "Computer illiterate"

She states: "You want your résumé to generate interest, not laughs: make sure it is error-free, and take time to step away from it before you proofread and do your final editing."

### Evaluate and Revise

✓ Evaluate your résumé. Consider both appearance and content.

### Print Your Résumé

You are at the final step. Don't blow it now. Have your résumé professionally printed or use a high-quality printer. Consider the following:

➤ Buy a quantity of blank 8 ½-by-11-inch white bond paper and matching 9 x 12 envelopes.
➤ Print only on one side and use black ink.
➤ Use a type that is easy to read, at least 10-point size, preferably 11- or 12-point.
➤ If necessary, slightly reduce the font size to assure adequate margins.
➤ Do NOT use all capital letters, script, bold or italic print. Use graphics sparingly or, better yet, not at all.
➤ Most people prefer a *serif* typestyle. Serifs are the little curves or feet added to the edges of letters to make them more readable. *Sans serif* typestyles do give a crisp, clean appearance, but are much harder to read. (Example: Arial Typeface—compare p and p, or A and A.

### Making it a "10"

Your résumé is a direct reflection of you on paper. Be sure it depicts you as you want—a professional for a professional job. Everything about your résumé will say something about *you*. Because employers have to start cutting back the number of finalists, they look for reasons *not* to pursue you as a candidate. For example, typos on a résumé have served as a legitimate reason for disregarding an application for any number of positions. Sometimes, when there are a lot of very good applicants, reasons for getting rid of one résumé and keeping another become, at best, arbitrary.

Put your résumé in an attractive binder or enclose it in an attractive envelope with the name and address of the prospective employer typed. This may say that this particular applicant put that extra effort into the process and should, therefore, be given consideration—an interview. Do not, however, use anything slippery or difficult to file. You don't want your résumé to stand out because it is hard to handle.

**The Cover Letter**

*Never* send a résumé without a cover letter, even if the employer has asked you to send a résumé. Cover letters should be individually typed, addressed to a specific person and company or department and signed. Anything less will be ineffective.

Keep your cover letter short and to the point. It is a brief personal introduction of the "you" embodied in your résumé. Don't repeat résumé information. Entice the reader to want to find out more about you. Make clear in your opening paragraph the type of résumé submission:

➢ Unsolicited. If so, give a reason for selecting this particular employer.

➢ Written as a referral or from personal contact, for example, "My mechanic told me your department was looking for qualified security officers."

➢ Written in response to a job advertisement.

Avoid starting every sentence with "I." *Never* start with: "I am writing this letter to apply for the job I saw advertised in the paper." BORING! Focus on the reader. More effective would be something like this: "Your opening for a police officer advertised in the *Gazette* is of great interest to me." Isaacs (20004a) offers the following advice about cover letters:

Your cover letter is the first thing employers see when they open your materials. Avoid these 10 mistakes, and make your first impression an impressive and lasting one.

**Don't Overuse "I."** Your cover letter is not your autobiography. The focus should be on how you meet an employer's needs, not on your life story. Avoid the perception of being self-centered by minimizing your use of the word "I," especially at the beginning of your sentences.

**Don't Use a Weak Opening.** Job seekers frequently struggle with the question of how to begin a cover letter. What results is often a feeble introduction lacking punch and failing to grab the reader's interest. Consider this example:

- **Weak:** Please consider me for your sales representative opening.
- **Better:** Your need for a top-performing sales representative is an excellent match to my three-year history as a #1 ranked multimillion-dollar producer.

**Don't Omit Your Top Selling Points.** A cover letter is a sales letter that sells you as a candidate. Just like the resume, it should be compelling and give the main reasons why you should be called for an interview. Winning cover letter strategies include emphasizing your top accomplishments or creating subheadings culled from the position ad. For example: "Your ad specifies…and I offer…"

**Don't Make It Too Long or Too Short.** If your cover letter is only one or two short paragraphs, it probably doesn't contain enough key information to sell you effectively. If it exceeds one page, you may be putting readers to sleep. Keep it concise but compelling, and be respectful of readers' time.

**Don't Repeat Your Resume Word-for-Word.** Your cover letter shouldn't just regurgitate what's on your resume. Reword your cover letter statements to avoid dulling your resume's impact.

**Don't Be Vague.** If you're replying to an advertised opening, reference the specific job title in your cover letter. The person reading your letter may be reviewing hundreds of letters for dozens of different jobs. Make sure all the content in your letter supports how you will meet the specific needs of the employer.

**Don't Forget to Customize.** If you're applying to a number of similar positions, chances are you're tweaking one letter and using it for multiple openings. That's fine, as long as you are customizing each one. Don't forget to update the company/job/contact information—if Mr. Jones is addressed as Mrs. Smith, he won't be impressed.

**Don't End on a Passive Note.** Put your future in your own hands with a promise to follow up. Instead of asking readers to call you, try a statement like this: I will follow up with you in a few days to answer any preliminary questions you may have. In the meantime, you may reach me at (555) 555-5555.

**Don't Be Rude.** Your cover letter should thank the reader for his time and consideration.

**Don't Forget to Sign the Letter.** It is proper business etiquette (and shows attention to detail) to sign your letter. However, if you are sending your cover letter and resume via e-mail or the Web, a signature isn't necessary.

Keep your letter short—one page. Be direct in requesting an interview. Send the letter to a specific person and use that individual's title. You can usually get this information by calling the agency or department, asking who is in charge of hiring and asking for the spelling of that person's name and official title. The little time this takes can pay big dividends.

As with your résumé, be sure to carefully proofread the cover letter. Morem (p. D2) reports: "A recent survey by the Society of Human Resource Management found that more than 80 percent of human resources professionals spend less than one minute reading a cover letter; 76 percent said a typo or grammatical error would remove an applicant for consideration."

An effective format for a cover letter is the full-block style—everything begins at the left margin. The parts of the letter should be as follows:

Your name
Your address (street number, street name and apartment
number, if applicable)
Your city, state and zip code
Your phone number(s) with area code
Your e-mail address

The date you are writing

The name of the person you are writing to
That person's title
The name of the company/department
The address of the employer

Salutation (Dear...):

Opening paragraph—why you are writing.

Second paragraph—provide some intriguing fact about
yourself as a lead into your résumé.

Concluding paragraph—ask for an interview and state where
you can be reached.

Complimentary closing (Sincerely, Yours truly),

(Skip four lines—sign in this space)

Typed name

Encl: Résumé

Notice the spacing between the various sections. Notice the capitalization
and the colon following the salutation and the comma following the
complimentary closing.

## Sending Your Résumé

Mail your cover letter and résumé unfolded in a 9 x 12 envelope. Everybody else's is going to be folded and crinkled. Résumés that travel flat are going to look better than all the others. As one employer commented: "When I looked for résumés, the easy ones to find are the flat ones. They stand out in the pile of folded résumés." Also, mail your letter and résumé to arrive in the employer's office on a Tuesday, Wednesday, or Thursday.

One final suggestion—consider using certified mail, with a return receipt requested. Not only will you eliminate those nagging doubts about if it got delivered, but again, it says something to the employer about the kind of person you are. Here is a candidate concerned enough to make *sure* it arrived. That's the kind of attention to detail a lot of employers are looking for.

## Electronic Submission and Faxing of Résumés

Sending material electronically is good—it makes a statement that you possess computer skills that today's employers desire—but keep the following in mind:

➢ Always keep a copy of anything you send, should you need it in the future.

➢ Make sure your electronic communiqués appear every bit as professional as those submitted in hardcopy. Begin with a proper salutation (Dear "recipient") and finish with a professional closing (Sincerely).

➢ Never use electronic communication simply because it is easier for you. Use it only because that is what is requested by the employer.

➢ Clearly state the purpose of your e-mail in the subject line (Application for job posting...). Never leave the subject line blank, as many antispam filters delete such "unannounced" e-mail. Furthermore, it may be considered rude or careless to not inform the recipient of the nature of your correspondence—they likely will not recognize your name and may simply delete the file without opening it.

➤ Do not assume electronic communications are always received. Glitches occur, servers go down, systems crash, antispam programs interfere—following up on all electronic correspondence is crucial in ensuring the intended recipient did, indeed, receive your material.

In the search for ways to get your résumé to prospective employers faster, it may be tempting to use a fax machine. And while fax and e-mail submissions are routine and acceptable for many employers, do not assume it is acceptable for all of them. You must ask first before you submit your résumé via fax machine. However, considering the relatively poor visual quality of most faxes as compared to e-mailed and printed documents and the increased likelihood of employers having e-mail capabilities, faxes now place a distant second to e-mail as a way to transmit documents instantaneously.

**Hand Delivering Your Résumé**

It's always a good idea to hand deliver a résumé if possible because it allows the employer to associate your name with a face. Dress well and look professional when you deliver your résumé. Even if you don't get to the boss, you will make a good impression on the staff person accepting it. These people can have a great deal of influence on their bosses. Don't let your guard down because you aren't dealing directly with upper management. When you drop your material off, it is another opportunity for you to emphasize that you really want the job. Keep in mind many secretaries and receptionists are gatekeepers. Establishing a positive contact with the person taking your résumé (or answering the phone) may also help you get that interview.

**Following Up**

Be sure to follow up. The follow-up is another opportunity to prove what kind of person you are—the kind they should hire! A day or two after you have mailed or hand delivered your résumé, write a brief letter to the employer. Recognize that the employer will be busy and only a short letter stands a chance of being read.

Confirm that you delivered your résumé and thank the employer for the opportunity to participate in the hiring process. Even if this merely gets stapled to your résumé without getting read initially by the employer, or gets forgotten by the employer who might read it, it is something that just might catch the attention of the interview committee when your résumé surfaces. If they are looking for reasons to keep some and get rid of others, this could be the reason yours stays in the running.

But *don't* become a pest. Too many letters or calls can just as easily land you in the "no" pile, identified as overly eager or unable to exercise enough common sense to know when it's "too much."

**For More Help**

Bookstores and libraries have dozens of texts on résumé writing, each with its own particular advice. Other sources of information and assistance may be found online—search under the keyword "résumé." The URLs and references below provide a start if you want to go into this topic in more detail or from other perspectives. If you are in college, your computer career center can be of help.

**Helpful Websites**

http://www.10minuteresume.com
http://www.eresumes.com
http://www.collegegrad.com

**References**

Barthel, Brea and Goldrick-Jones, Amanda. The Writing Center, Rensselaer Polytechnic Institute. Online: http://www.rpi.edu/web/writingcenter/resume.html

Challenger, John A. "Surprise! Resume Rules Have Changed.*" Bottom Line Personal*, March 15, 2000, p. 6.

Hayes, Kit Harrington. "Scannable Resumes." *Bottom Line Personal*, September 15, 2000, p. 15.

Hofferber, Karen. "Breaking Tradition with a Functional Resume." Monster Career Center, 2004. Online: http://resume.monster.com/articles/functionalresume

Isaacs, Kim. "Ten Cover Letter Don'ts." Monster Career Center, 2004a. Online: http://resume.monster.com/coverletter/donot/

Isaacs, Kim. "Tips for Creating A Scannable Resume." Monster Career Center, 2004b. Online: http://resume.monster.com/articles/scannableresume/

JobWeb. Online: http://www.jobweb.com/resumes_interviews/resume_guide/res.htm

*Land That Job!* Online: http://www.landjob.com

Morem, Sue. "Don't Make Mistake of Erring with Résumé." (Minneapolis/St. Paul) *Star Tribune*, November 13, 2001, p. D2.

Newfield, Peter. "Ten Resume 'Don'ts'." Monster Career Center, 2004. Online: http://resume.monster.com/dosanddonts/resumedonts

Parker, Yana. *Damn Good Resume Guide*. Online: http://www.damngood.com

Razek, Rula. "Setting Your Sites on Finding a New Job." *USA Weekend*, August 31-September 2, 2001, p. 12.

*Resume.com.* Online: http://www.resume.com

*Resume Logic*: Online: http://www.resumelogic.com/index.htm

# CHAPTER SIX

# THINK BEFORE YOU SPEAK:
# THE VERBAL COMPONENT

*A marked departure in foreign policy was observed at the beginning of George W. Bush's administration. While former President Clinton had promoted reaching an agreement with North Korea that would have ended its development and export of ballistic missiles and related technologies, Bush expressed criticism. In addition, National Security Advisor Condoleeza Rice described North Korea as the "roadkill of history[1]." However, Security of State Colin Powell, when questioned about the administration's policies, stated that "we do plan to engage with North Korea to pick up where President Clinton and his administration left off. Some promising elements were left on the table and we will be examining those elements.[2]" While apparently part of the same administration, these three individuals clearly expressed differing ideas regarding foreign policy concerning North Korea.*

Even though its name implies speech, verbal communication actually consists of all oral *and* written communications. The life and work of a criminal justice professional involves both aspects of oral and written communication. Preparing reports that are grammatically sound while providing all essential information is an imperative. By the same token, the oral component of verbal communication requires careful planning and thoughtful preparation prior to speaking.

## Verbal Communication: The Oral Component

Consider how limited we would be as a society if we could not verbally ask questions or give instructions. Oral communication is the only way we have of receiving immediate answers to questions or of providing feedback to others. How would you know if you had performed a job well or if you required further information if you and others around you could not speak? Another facet of oral communication involves listening skills. Speaking and listening are reciprocal parts of the communication process.

| Three Myths of Listening[3] | Three Truths of Listening |
|---|---|
| Listening cannot be learned; it is a natural occurrence. | Listening is not a natural activity; it is learned. |
| Hearing and listing are the same. | Telling someone something is not the same thing as communicating. |
| When you speak, everyone listens. | You speak to one person at a time ?  even in an audience situation. |

### Listening

Just as important to the oral component of communication as the spoken word is our ability to listen. Listening skills are vital in any profession, but in matters of law enforcement, listening effectively is a top priority. Consider that on average, we remember approximately 25 percent of what we hear in any conversation. If we remember only one-fourth of the information, then three-fourths of the content of that conversation is lost.

Listening and speaking are part of a natural process that should occur together. Most of the time we converse and listen; rarely are we required to do only one or the other. Five concepts of listening underscore the reciprocity involved in speaking and listening: **attending, understanding, remembering, analyzing critically,** and **responding empathically.**[3]

The **attending** concept of listening refers to the process of selecting or focusing on specific stimuli from amongst the countless number of stimuli we receive. In order to effectively listen, the attending process gives us parameters to follow.

1.     Prepare yourself, both physically and mentally, to listen. Compel
       yourself to focus on what is being said.
2.     Give the speaker the appropriate time to complete his/her
       statement(s) before you react. In other words, do not rehearse what
       you are planning to say in response to something the speaker said–
       LISTEN to what is being said until the speaker's intent is
       complete.
3.     Adjust your listening to the goal of the situation. Determine the
       goal of your communication. Do you need to understand, to
       evaluate, to respond, or to comfort? Depending on your goal in the
       communication situation, your listening will range from "pleasure
       listening" (i.e., listening without much intensity) to "critical
       analysis."

A second aspect of listening is **understanding**. When we decode (or
translate) a message accurately by assigning appropriate meaning to it, we
are able to understand the message. To fully understand what another
individual says requires **active listening**. When we engage in active
listening, we use specific techniques of empathizing, asking questions, and
paraphrasing. More discussion on active listening will follow later in this
chapter.

**Remembering**, the third concept of listening, is being able to process
information and store it for later retrieval (or recall). Unfortunately, our
ability to remember is very limited. Often we cannot remember the name of
a person to whom we have been introduced merely moments earlier. Several
techniques are available which can assist us in remembering information:
repetition, mnemonics, and taking notes.

1.     **Repetition** helps listeners store information in long-term memory.
       Repetition refers to saying something two, three, or even four times
       to reinforce the information. If we do not engage in repetition,
       whatever we hear will be held in short-term memory for
       approximately 20 seconds and then discarded.
2.     Constructing **mnemonics** is another technique we can use to help
       us remember information. "A mnemonic device is any artificial
       technique used as a memory aid" (Verderber, 1999, p. 141). When
       attempting to remember items in a sequence, you can try to form a

sentence using the words themselves, or you can take the first letter of a list of items you are trying to remember and form a word.

3. **Note taking** provides an additional venue for retaining information. While you would not want to take notes during a casual interpersonal encounter, telephone conversations, interviews, interrogations, etc., would benefit from this powerful tool for increasing your recall of information.

**Critical analysis**, the fourth concept of listening, is the process you engage in when attempting to determine whether information you hear is truthful, authentic, or believable. Critical analysis requires you to be able to distinguish between facts and inferences. You also have to be able to evaluate the quality of inferences. **Factual statements** can be verified or proven. **Inferences**, on the other hand, are assertions or claims that are based on observation or fact but that are not necessarily true. As an effective listener, you have to be able to distinguish between statements that can be accepted at face value as truths and statements that require proof (inferences).

The final concept of listening involves **responding empathically**. When we respond empathically to give comfort, we are indicating that we have understood a person's meaning but also affirming that the person has a right to his or her own feelings. Offering support to others shows that we care about them and what happens to them. As an effective listener, you will want to offer supporting statements to demonstrate that you empathize with the person's feelings, regardless of intensity or direction.

**The Listening Process**

We are taught as young children that listening is a passive activity that requires no effort on our part. Our educational institutions, families, etc., condition us to believe that we do not need to work at listening. Remember when you were in elementary school and the teacher gave you an assignment? That assignment would most likely be repeated several times or in frustration, the teacher would simply write it on the board to avoid the need to repeat it. Your parents would often have to call you several times for dinner or remind you repeatedly to take out the garbage or to clean your room. When confronted about your behavior, you might even have said, "I didn't hear you."

Listening and Hearing. Is there a difference between **hearing** and **listening**? **Hearing** involves the perception of sound; a physiological process whereby sound waves strike the eardrum and cause vibrations that travel to the brain.[4] **Listening** means we attach a meaning to the sounds that have been transmitted to our brain. When we listen, we go beyond the sound itself. We discern various sounds and ideas and comprehend and attach meanings to them. Listening, therefore, is an active skill.

Much like speaking, reading, or writing, listening requires us to be engaged both physically and psychologically. Physical responses to listening involve an increased pulse rate, higher blood pressure, and a slight elevation in body temperature. When counselors and negotiators proclaim that they are exhausted at the end of a day's work, they are merely stating a fact. Their responses to the listening process have effectively rendered them physically drained—much as if they had been performing a type of manual labor.

Psychological responses to listening are much harder to identify. Since we each have our own beliefs or perceptions of the world, we find it difficult (sometimes impossible) to truly listen to others. If listening to another means that we would have to change, most of us would prefer to maintain the status quo and to avoid a variation in our beliefs. After all, change is frightening; so listening could involve considerable risk that we would have to examine what we think or feel and perhaps how we act.

Types of Listening. Three general types of listening have been consistently noted in research. However, the level or intensity of listening activity in which you engage varies with the conversation topic, the relevancy of the subject matter to your needs, and the people involved in the conversation. The three types of listening are **casual or marginal listening, attentive listening**, and **active listening**[5].

**Casual or marginal listening** occurs when listening is secondary in importance to some other activity in which you are engaged. The listener in this situation is not required to learn, comprehend, or remember any materials for later recall and action. An example might be the off-duty police officer that has a scanner running in his home. The officer is not actively listening to what is being said on the scanner when he is engaged in watching television or interacting with his family; he simply has the scanner on in the background. A similar scenario would occur when an individual is driving to work with the radio on in the car. The major focus would be on driving and watching for other vehicles, not on listening to what is being said on the radio.

**Attentive listening** occurs when there is a need to obtain some information that might be required for a future action. To follow through with the example of the off-duty police officer and his scanner, if he is watching television and suddenly he hears an emergency come through such as "officer needs assistance" or "officer down, needs assistance," then he would suddenly be compelled to listen attentively to the scanner to determine the location of the officer in trouble. The scenario where the individual is driving to work and listening to the radio could become one requiring attentive listening if an emergency broadcast were suddenly to be issued. The driver would then be motivated to hear, understand, and remember what was being said in the broadcast.

The final type of listening is **active listening**. This type of listening occurs most frequently in counseling, interviewing, and interrogating situations. In these situations you are required to listen for more than just the words or the content of the message. You need to pay attention to the nonverbal language and emotions of the speaker. Active listening is most difficult because it requires you to put aside personal preferences and to physically and psychologically listen.

Active listening also requires you to demonstrate four types of behavior: **acceptance, congruence, empathy,** and **concreteness. Acceptance** says to the speaker that the listener will not pass judgment or will not criticize the speaker. An important first step in getting a speaker to trust you is to demonstrate acceptance. Once the speaker trusts you, he or she will feel free to share feelings or thoughts.

**Congruence** is defined as agreeing or harmonizing. In active listening, congruence refers to the agreement or harmony between the speaker's experience, the way he or she feels about the experience, and what the speaker then conveys to others about that experience. In law enforcement, a sergeant is required to take the lieutenant's examination to be placed in line for promotion. For example, Sergeant Mary Smith takes the exam and achieves a score of 93. She is ranked number one in the line for promotion to lieutenant. When the next available lieutenant's slot opens, the sergeant is promoted. She has worked very hard for this promotion and feels very good about it. As a result, Sergeant Smith tells her friends and co-workers about the promotion and how excited she is. At this point, there is total harmony between her experience, her feelings, and her communication to others. As an active listener, you have to be aware of the congruence or absence of congruence in a speaker. When congruence is not present—when no harmony exists between the speaker's experience and feelings, communication will not take place.

In active listening, congruence becomes problematic when an individual is lacking harmony or agreement in his or her experience, feelings, and communication. To use the foregoing example, if Sergeant Smith were to be passed over for the promotion and the person who was ranked second were to be promoted in her place, she would find it very difficult to assist the new lieutenant with his or her duties. Sergeant Smith would be angry that her belief in hard work was ill founded. She would then find it difficult to listen to the new lieutenant when he or she discussed loyalty and duty among the department.

**Empathy** refers to "putting yourself in another's position." In order to be empathetic toward another, you must attempt to vicariously experience his or her feelings, thoughts, and emotions. When a listener is successful in practicing empathy, he or she is better able to respond appropriately to the concerns or needs of the speaker. Empathy is particularly important in situations of cultural diversity. We must learn to subordinate our opinions and emotions and to approach situations with an open mind. This task is especially difficult given our tendency as humans to judge people. However, the only way to be successful in communication is to listen with empathy.

The final critical behavior for active listening is **concreteness**. Concreteness refers to the speaker's need to concentrate on actions over which he or she has control. We have all heard statements such as "I don't know what to do about Mary. She used to be such a good worker." Nothing the speaker says here has any specific meaning. An active listener would encourage the speaker to give definitive statements about the problem with Mary's work. In this way, a plan of action can be formulated to help Mary work through whatever issues are involved in the situation.

## Types of Ineffective Listeners[6]

Through research, we have come to recognize several types of listeners: the **faker**, the **continual talker**, the **rapid-writing note taker**, the **critic**, the **"I'm in a hurry"** the **"hand on the doorknob,"** the **"make sure it is correct,"** the **"finish the sentence for you,"** and the **"I've done one better,"** listeners. Each of these listeners has characteristics you will recognize from your own or others' actions.

| Type of Listener | Characteristics |
|---|---|
| **The Critic** | • Listens merely for points of fact which he or she can take issue with.<br>• Waits only to hear something that he or she finds emotionally charged and then proceeds to formulate a mental argument, neglecting to continue listening to the speaker. |
| **The Faker** | • Appears for all intents and purposes to be paying close attention to what is being said.<br>• Nods his or her head at all the right places, makes appropriate eye contact, and appears to be following the conversation closely.<br>• In reality, this type of listener is merely faking-- doing what is necessary to convince another that he or she is listening intently. |
| **The Continual Talker** | • Find it very difficult to listen to anyone since they never stop talking!<br>• Always has something to say, interrupts conversations to talk, and rarely allows anyone else to contribute to the conversation. |
| **The I'm in a Hurry** | • Too busy to stop whatever he or she is doing and look at the speaker.<br>• Usually performs some other task while "listening"? shuffling papers on a desk, searching for a lost object, etc. |
| **The Make Sure it is Correct** | • The person who listens for facts and will be the first to point out mistakes or errors. |

| | |
|---|---|
| | • Seems to thrive on pointing out the mistakes of others. <br> • Will interrupt in order to make a point and cause the speaker to look bad. |
| **The I've Done One Better** | • Listens only for the points of action in a story and then proceeds to intrude with statements of his or her own. <br> • Always climbed a higher mountain, captured a more violent criminal, drove faster in a high-speed chase, etc., than the speaker. <br> • Doesn't really process what the speaker has said since he or she believes that the speaker's story is not nearly as good as his or her own. |
| **The Hand on the Doorknob** | • Always in a hurry and has little time to waste listening. <br> • He or she will signal when the conversation is at an end by reaching for the doorknob or placing his or her materials away, regardless of whether or not the speaker has actually completed the conversation. <br> • Once the listener has indicated that he or she has finished listening, to continue speaking would be futile–nothing is penetrating the "hand on the doorknob" listener's brain. |
| **The Finish the Sentence For You** | • Will intrude on a speaker to complete the sentence if the speaker pauses. <br> • Impatient <br> • Sure he or she knows what the speaker was going to say next. |
| **The Rapid– Writing Note Taker** | • Attempts to write everything down that is being said. <br> • In attempting to write verbatim what the speaker has said, this individual misses the entire point of the conversation. In the legal field, court reporters are charged with creating verbatim transcripts of depositions, testimony at trials and hearings, and sworn |

| | statements. However, other than this profession, few exist which require individuals to write down everything that is being said. |
| | • In attempting to write down everything in a presentation or conversation, this listener is missing the main points because he or she is so busy writing that he or she does not have the mental capacity to process the information. |

## Barriers to Listening

<u>Mental and emotional distractions</u>. One of the greatest deterrents to listening involves mental distractions. We can comprehend information at a rate three times that at which most people speak. Because we have a "gap" between the time the words are spoken and the time we hear and process them, we have a tendency to let our thoughts drift. We take a mental vacation, perhaps picturing ourselves lying on the beach in the warm sunshine, or tallying a list of items we need to get done today, or even preparing for our next meeting or activity. While we wander away from the speaker, we often lose track of what is being said and have trouble returning our concentration to the matter at hand. Consequently, we find that our efficiency as listeners is very low. In fact, we forget as much as 80 percent of what we hear within the first 24 hours of hearing it.

Emotional distractions are very similar to mental distractions. However, emotional distractions refer more to our overreaction to the words or message that the speaker is delivering. Each of us has a "buzz" word that is capable of diverting our attention away from the message. We then concentrate on the word or phrase and become so preoccupied that we neglect the speaker. A police officer that detests being called a "pig" would become incensed by a perpetrator's use of the term in an interrogation. The question and answer session would be hindered by the officer's emotional response to the use of the word "pig."

<u>Common frame of reference</u>. Another barrier to effective listening stems from the absence of a common frame of reference. The speaker and the listener must have a level of shared knowledge. In other words, they must

have a common vocabulary. A probation and parole officer, if using legal terminology, would find it difficult to speak with an individual unfamiliar with the court system. For that reason, the officer would have to use words or phrases common to the individual.

Physical distractions. We have all been in situations where the room was too warm, the noise in the hall outside the door was too loud, or where our stomach was growling from hunger. These are physical distractions that impede our ability to listen actively. Even though it may be difficult to return to listening following one of these physical disruptions, we should try to consciously move back to the speaker as quickly as possible.

Evaluation/Judgment. Unfortunately, we as human beings have a tendency to judge others by their appearance, opinions, or knowledge. Even though we know that you "can't judge a book by its cover," we still make assumptions about others without knowing all the facts. When we make a rush to judge someone, we cease to listen to anything that person has to say. In effect, we shut down and close our minds.

Miscellaneous. Several conditions also exist which might affect our ability to listen. Examples of these conditions are
- ? our interest in the topic or activity
- ? our attitude toward the presenter and subject
- ? any distractions we face, whether emotional, mental, or physical
- ? the nonverbal behavior of the speaker
- ? the time of day for the activity or presentation

**Guidelines for Effective Listening**

Instruction in listening skills has been neglected in our educational institutions. As mentioned earlier, if we are taught anything about listening, we are taught that we **really don't have to listen**. Educational facilities need to incorporate programs of instruction in listening. However, we may still acquire good listening skills on our own. Some steps for improving your listening ability are as follows:

> **Stop Talking!** Remember, you cannot listen if you have your mouth open.

- ➤ **Pay Attention!** Give your full attention to the speaker. You cannot communicate if both parties are not actively involved in the process.

- ➤ **Read Nonverbal Cues.** Along with hearing and processing the words of the speaker, you should pay careful attention to the nonverbal language being communicated. Watch for eye contact, expressions, gestures, and so on.

- ➤ **Ask Questions.** A good way to ensure that you have accurately understood the message is to ask questions of the speaker.

- ➤ **Resist Distractions.** Stop doodling! Do not shuffle papers, draw, or doodle when you are listening.

- ➤ **Don't Interrupt!** Even though you may get angry or upset by something the speaker says, do not interrupt. Let the speaker finish and resist the temptation to focus on your emotional response to the speaker's words.

- ➤ **Open your Mind.** Try to look at the situation from the speaker's point of view and not just your own. Be flexible.

- ➤ **Paraphrase.** Use your own words to mirror what you have heard. Restating information in your own words helps you to remember what you have heard.

## Criminal Justice Professionals and Oral Communication

Criminal justice professionals are involved in five primary areas of oral communication: responding, reporting, interviewing, interrogating, and testifying. Each area has both a formal and an informal aspect. In the same vein, each component may be delegated to a different level of supervision within the agency. For instance, only in the most extreme cases, or in very small agencies, would the Chief of Police be involved in a suspect interview and/or interrogation. By the same token, rarely do patrol officers make presentations to the city council or mayor. However, every member of a law enforcement agency should be able to speak publicly and to present the agency in the best light possible.

## Responding

Two methods are employed for responding to complaints or inquiries from the general public: formal and informal. These responses are also ascribed a certain priority depending upon the nature of the complaint and, unfortunately, the status of the complainant.

The most common type of citizen inquiry or complaint is one made to the chief of police concerning either a local problem (i.e., parking on the street in neighborhoods, barking dogs, etc.) or a complaint about an officer's conduct or behavior. Generally, these issues necessitate a formal written response from the chief or corresponding head of the local law enforcement agency. The chief or other agency head will usually delegate this matter to a first-line supervisor (sergeant) for investigation. However, if the complaint or inquiry is of an extremely sensitive nature, it may be delegated to a mid-level manager or shift commander (lieutenant).

The investigation then follows an established procedure whereby the investigating officer will frequently travel to the area to observe firsthand the nature of the complaint, if possible. This visit may include a personal contact with the complainant as well as interviews with witnesses or neighbors affected by the complaint. The officer will review the local ordinance and/or law specific to the complaint, if such exists, and offer an opinion based upon the officer's interpretation of the statute. At this point, the investigating officer will prepare a formal written report to the chief detailing the findings and analysis of the problem. The officer may make a recommendation based upon a careful examination of the issue. The report is then forwarded to the chief who will review the provided information, formulate an opinion, and prepare a written response to the complainant's inquiry or complaint. The chief is the only person who will issue an official response to the complaint or inquiry.

Informal complaints are generally handled via the telephone or by personal contact with a local or district patrol officer. These issues may be just as significant to the complainant; however, they do not carry the same sense of importance since they are not in written form. Some of the informal issues police officers are asked to resolve involve alien abductions, directions to certain locations, requirements for becoming a police officer, and other sometimes amusing requests. Frequently, the officer will make a spontaneous decision concerning the nature of the problem and the best manner in which to resolve the issue. If the complainant initiates no further contact, the officer considers the problem to have been solved.

**Verbal Communication: The Written Component**

As explained earlier in this chapter, verbal communication is comprised of two parts—oral and written. Writing is more difficult than speaking because you do not have access to immediate feedback. In essence, you have to be able to communicate your message without the benefit of being able to see the person with whom you are communicating. Written communication may take the form of letters, memoranda, e-mail, or reports. Each of these types of messages has an appropriate use and a corresponding purpose.

1. **Letters**. Letters are used to communicate outside the agency. Typically a criminal justice agency will have an existing letterhead on which all letters must be typed.
2. **Memoranda**. A memorandum is a written message used to communicate within the agency. Traditionally, a memorandum includes the headings "To," "From," "Date," and "Subject."
3. **E-Mail** (electronic mail). E-mail is a message transmitted electronically via the use of a computer network. E-mail may be sent either within the agency or outside the agency. E-mail's appearance is very similar to a memorandum with the same headings, "To," "From," "Date," and "Subject." E-mail should be given the same considerations as other forms of communication. The rules of grammar, punctuation, and spelling also apply to E-mail.
4. **Reports**. Reports are documents written in an organized manner used to communicate findings or developments and to provide updates for projects, etc.

While oral communication is important in obtaining and maintaining interest, the written document serves as a permanent record for others to review in the future. In the criminal justice profession, written documentation is vital to the success of any agency.

**Writing Techniques: Choosing the Right Words**

Our choice of words in written documentation is very important to the effective transfer of information. Improper or inappropriate word choice can hinder even the best attempt at communication. The following principles of word choice should guide you in developing your written documentation.

1.  **Write clearly.** You must write in a complete, accurate manner. Give the reader a message he or she can understand and act on.

    A.  <u>Accuracy</u>. As a writer, you must use your integrity to make sure your communications are ethical. Your credibility is the most important facet in communication with others, and if you damage or destroy the trust of your reader through misleading information, you may never be able to repair the damage.

    B.  <u>Completeness</u>. Your message must contain all necessary information for the reader to make an informed decision. A good place for you as the writer to start is to develop the five **W's**: who, what, when, where, and why.

    C.  <u>Jargon and Word Familiarity</u>. Every field has its own special vocabulary. When communicating with others in your area, the use of jargon is appropriate. However, you should remember that the use of jargon is inappropriate when you are writing for the reader outside your agency. You should strive as a writer to use terms that are familiar both to you and to your reader.

2.  **Use Simple Words**. Using long words in communication is not necessary to achieve your purpose. Short, simple words are a better choice. Your reader is less likely to become confused when you opt for words that convey the precise meaning you desire. You want your readers to focus on the information you are presenting, not on the words themselves.

3. **Use Concrete Language**. Concrete words give the reader a mental picture of what you mean in your writing. Try to avoid using words such as *several, a number of, a few, a lot of, substantial*, etc. Give definite numbers or specific information.

4. **Avoid the Use of Clichés and Slang**. A **cliché** is an expression that has been overused in our language. Examples might consist of "according to our records," "if you have any further questions," "if I may be of further assistance," "please find enclosed," etc. **Slang** is informal word usage usually identified with a specific group of people. For this reason, you should avoid the use of slang in your writing.

5. **Avoid Wordiness**. Because people are exceedingly busy in today's society, you should strive to be concise in your writing. When one or two words will suffice, why would you use four or more to say, in effect, the same thing? Examples of excessive wordiness would be "enclosed herewith," "enclosed you will find," "a long period of time," "continuous and uninterrupted," and others.

6. **Use Positive Language**. You are more likely to build goodwill with your reader if you write using positive as opposed to negative language. You should attempt to avoid the use of negative or negative-sounding words in your writing. For example, eliminate or minimize the use of words like *cannot, will not, failure, refuse, deny, mistake*, etc.

## Developing and Writing Effective Sentences and Paragraphs

In addition to selecting appropriate words, using a variety of sentences in your writing is important to the complete development of logical paragraphs. When we vary our sentence types between simple, compound, and complex, we keep our writing interesting and our reader interested.

> ➤ A **simple sentence** is one in which you present a single idea.
> ➤ A **compound sentence** contains two or more independent clauses, each of which presents a complete idea.
> ➤ A **complex sentence** contains one independent clause and at least one dependent clause. Typically the dependent

clauses present additional information that is not as
important as that contained in the independent clause.

A **paragraph** is defined as a group of sentences that focus on one main idea
or topic. Paragraphs must be unified and give information which is directly
related to the topic. This information must be organized in a logical manner
and contain all relevant details. Paragraphs also must be cohesive. That is,
they must integrate the words together in such a way as to create a
relationship between the sentences. Transitional words should be used to
join sentences for a step-by-step movement. These "road signs" tell your
reader where your message is heading.

You should attempt to control the length of your paragraphs so that you
have enough information to support your main idea or topic, but not so long
that your important information or ideas get buried in the middle of a long
block of unbroken text. Effective paragraphs typically fall somewhere
between the 60 to 80 word range.

---

**Transitional Expressions**

also, besides, furthermore, in addition, moreover, too, as a
result, because, consequently, hence, so, therefore, thus,
likewise, although, nevertheless, still, for example, in other
words, at last, finally, in conclusion, meanwhile, since, next

---

**Criminal Justice Professionals and Written Communication**

Reporting

The situation or scenario of reporting in a paramilitary organization can be
one of the most delicate and politically sensitive actions taken by an agency
member. No matter what position you occupy in the chain of command,
reporting can always be filled with hazards. The individual department
member needs to be aware of the nature of the reporting situation and
whether it is formal or informal.

Generally when making a report, the recipient is a "higher" authority in the
chain of command. Therefore, the presenter is put at a psychological

disadvantage in this reporting situation. For that reason, the presenter must be prepared and rehearsed, when possible. The agency member should be aware of the topic for discussion prior to the actual formal meeting and should attempt to control the environment in which the reporting occurs. In addition to giving the advantage to the presenter, this allows time to properly prepare the report and to rehearse the presentation. The presenter should pay particular attention to any areas that may be sensitive or offensive to the recipient. While certain comments may seem innocuous to the presenter, they may produce or provoke an inadvertent response. An example might occur when an officer must report to the shift commander regarding matters of impropriety with respect to gender or ethnic issues. In this scenario, the officer must be cognizant of the lieutenant's biases in these areas. Occasions have arisen in which inadvertent remarks later impacted an officer's opportunities for promotion or transfer. Every opportunity should be taken to eliminate biased or sexist language from the vocabulary.

Testifying

> *"In the Fall of 1990, before the Senate Judiciary Committee, chaired by Joseph Biden, when queried on his response to casual drug users, Chief Gates responded the casual drug user ought to be taken out and shot."*
>
> . . . .
>
> *"They ought to be taken out and shot because if this is a war on drugs, they are giving aid and comfort to the enemy."*[7]

Testifying is a recitation of facts or information, under oath, gained during the course of an investigation. Testifying usually involves only those facts of which the officer has direct knowledge. However, in some instances, under specific guidelines officers are allowed to proffer an opinion. Law enforcement officials may be called upon to testify in courtroom proceedings, in depositions, and in sworn statements. Furthermore, in certain select instances, criminal justice professionals may be called upon to testify before governmental bodies such as the Senate Judiciary Committee mentioned in the quote above.

The Officer Speaks in the Courtroom. When an officer testifies in court, he/she is in a confrontational setting. Obviously, the defendant's attorney, in an attempt to seek the best defense possible for his/her client, is going to question the officer's recollection of the facts, gathering of the evidence, procedural propriety, or professional integrity. Frequently, the officer is at a distinct disadvantage in the courtroom setting from an educational standpoint. The major participants in the courtroom all have law degrees or three years' post-graduate education while the typical police officer has a high school diploma or, at most, an associate's degree from a local community college.

Any discrepancy noted in the officer's written reports or testimony will be thoroughly examined. When testifying in a court action, an officer must carefully review all materials prior to taking the stand. Oftentimes, the officer will be prepared by the prosecuting attorney for the types of questions he/she can expect to be asked both by the prosecution and by the defense. The officer has the opportunity to cast him/herself in the best light possible at this point by being prepared.

The Officer gives a Deposition. The courtroom is the legal arena for fact-finding and the determination of guilt or innocence. A deposition, however, is an opportunity for discovery or a "fishing" expedition. The latitude in a sworn deposition with regard to questioning is much broader in scope. Queries made of the officer need not be limited to the parameters of the case at hand. Therefore, an officer's performance in previous cases, matters of professional or career development (with particular regard to previous disciplinary actions due to poor performance or inappropriate behavior), and matters involving an officer's personal life are all open for examination in a deposition. Delving into the officer's life in this way is an attempt to discover any biases or prejudices, which would alter or affect his/her testimony or perception of facts as they relate to the case.

Depositions are stress inducing and frequently confrontational in nature. Even the most patient officer may find that a deposition tests the limits of that patience.

The Officer makes a Sworn Statement. Sworn statements are typically written documents that serve in lieu of an officer's personal appearance in a legal proceeding.

**Verbal Communication: The Video Component**

Up to this point, the discussion has focused on face-to-face verbal communication. Face-to-face communication is indicative of the old adage, "You can't unring a bell." Once a statement has been made in a one-on-one situation, the information can never be retrieved nor the statement recanted. However, in videotaped communications, the opportunity exists for misstatements or faux pas to be retaped prior to distribution.

While law enforcement officials predominantly rely on face-to-face communication, certain instances exist in which videotaped presentations are more efficient and most cost effective. This is particularly true with regard to training tapes. With the increase in costs associated with training and given that training is essential due to the high incidence of litigation against law enforcement agencies, training tapes are vital to insulating a department against excessive civil judgments.

Training tapes are routinely prepared or created by officers who have a certain area of expertise. Training tapes are also generated quite by accident through the recording of officer/citizen interaction on the street. The use of these tapes allows training officers to continue with their normal duties rather than having to interrupt a busy schedule to instruct in the academy. Furthermore, if travel is involved, these tapes eliminate the costs associated with transportation, room and board for the sponsoring department.

Aside from training tapes, recorded prepared statements to the news media are often used to inform the public of ongoing investigations or critical incidents. The advantage of using recorded statements is that the officer is given the opportunity to review a list of questions the media will ask, to prepare appropriate responses, and to rehearse those responses. The officer must confine his/her responses to only those questions that have been previously submitted. He/She should not attempt to or be lured into responding to questions outside the scope of the current issue. Spontaneity at this point could be extremely detrimental to the integrity of the investigation or the reputation of the department.

On occasion, officers are confronted by news media at the scene of a crime or critical incident. At this point, no opportunity for advance preparation is present. Therefore, the officer must be extremely guarded in his/her response to questions from the media. Officers should inform the media that the investigation is in the preliminary stages and specific details at this time are not available or may serve as a barrier to a successful investigation. The officer should attempt to be candid in his/her statements, but should not allow the media to force a hasty or inappropriate response. Officers need to be wary of the "60 second sound bite." Some reporters or news agencies will attempt to create or capture a headline in order to make the early evening or late news.

Regardless of whether the interview situation is spontaneous or planned, the responding officer should maintain proper decorum and adhere to the fundamentals of proper speech. A short film clip provides the opportunity for an officer to greatly enhance or to rapidly destroy the image of the department due to the tremendous number of viewers. More damage can occur in that 30-second sound bite than the department could incur in 30 years of service to the public. Unfortunately, the adage that may be most appropriate is "often an ounce of perception is worth a pound of performance." Following the guidelines for effective oral presentations affords opportunities for the law enforcement community to enhance its image. As important as good oral communication skills are, communication is a bi-fold process involving both verbal and nonverbal skills. If what the officer says is contradicted by inappropriate nonverbal cues, then the officer's credibility is questioned.

**Summary**

Verbal communication involves both the oral and written facets of communication. Oral communication is a reciprocal process that involves both listening and speaking. Listening is a vitally important skill because we get the information we need to cope with our environment through listening. However, hearing and listening are not synonymous terms. Hearing involves the physiological response to sound while listening is both physical and psychological processing of sound. Many barriers exist to listening, but we should try to overcome our tendency to close our minds to new information.

The written aspect of verbal communication typically involves the preparation of letters, memoranda, e-mail, and reports. In our writing, we should remember to choose our words carefully, trying to maintain clarity and conciseness in our selections. The reader must be able to understand our message, and he or she will not be able to do so if we use jargon or slang inappropriately.

Sentences and paragraphs are important to the logical transfer of information. Simply choosing the appropriate word will not suffice when preparing written communication. Our sentences must vary in length between simple, compound, and complex styles; and our paragraphs should logically develop our main idea or topic while holding to a 60 to 80-word maximum. We should remember to use transitional words in paragraph development so that our sentences flow in a progressive and understandable manner.

**Notes**

1. "Bush Shows Cold Shoulder Across the Pacific." Guardian Unlimited. (n.d.). September 3, 2002 <http://www.guardian.co.uk/korea/article>.
2. "Missile Negotiations." Center for Arms Control and Non-proliferation. (n.d.). September 3, 2002
<http://www.armscontrolcenter.org/prolifproject/southeast_asia>.
4. Verderber, R. F., *Communication in Our Lives*. Belmont, CA: Wadsworth, 1999, pp. 130-155.
5. Wood, J. T., *Communication in Our Lives*. Belmont, CA: Wadsworth, 1997, p. 95.
6. Wood, J. T., pp.110-115.
7. Johnson, I.W., and Pearce, C. G., "Assess and Improve your Listening Quotient." *Business Education Forum*, March 1990, pp. 22-27.
8. Gates, D., *Chief: My Life in the LAPD*. Los Angeles: Bantam Books, 1992, p. 286.

# PART IV

## *POLICE REPORT WRITING*

# CHAPTER SEVEN

# THE PROCESS OF REPORT WRITING

Human memory is not perfect. It is usually necessary to take notes of events we wish to later recall exactly. These notes are often referred to as field notes because they are made "in the field." Field notes are mere abbreviations of what was actually said, seen or done because few of us can write all things down as quickly as we hear, see or do them.

Field notes are primarily for the use of the reporting officer, not the prosecuting attorney, judge or jury. Field notes are, therefore, the exception to the rule concerning writing public safety reports in complete sentences with standard abbreviations. Just as you take lecture notes that are not complete sentences in class to later refresh your memory before a test, you take field notes to later refresh your memory when writing reports.

Ever try to use someone else's class notes? Weren't you frustrated if you couldn't understand them or thankful if you could? Though non-standard abbreviations and non-sentences may be used in field notes, make sure at least some other officer can understand them in case something happens to you.

Good field notes help eliminate the need to re-contact the parties involved just as good class notes help the need to later ask your instructors about earlier lectures.

Because of the imperfection of human memory, good field notes (or good class notes) will provide better recollection than mere memory alone.

What types of information should be included in field notes? What types of things will you later need for writing your report? Minimally, your field notes will need to include information about:

**Suspects** *(What are their names? addresses? descriptions?)*

**Victims** *(You need work **and** home information for detectives and subpoenas.)*

**Witnesses** *(Virtually the same information needed for victims is needed for witnesses.)*

**Date(s) and time(s) of occurrence** *(It happened between when and when?)*

**Exact location of occurrence** *(Necessary to establish jurisdiction and possible later crime scene or accident reconstruction.)*

**Any other important information** *(You can't include **everything** but you'll* never have a better chance to get all important information than that first time at the scene. When in doubt, make an error of too much information instead of too *little.)*

When interviewing people in the field, put them at ease. Establish rapport if time allows by showing some personal interest in them. Try to become a person to them, not just an officer.

**EXAMPLES**

**Ask:** Would you be more comfortable sitting down? (*This **asking**, as opposed to **ordering**, helps eliminate the intimidating effect of the badge and uniform.)*

**Explain:** I know you're a bit shaken by this but the information I need from you might help us recover your property and catch the thief. *(Explaining your purpose and showing concern for a victim's feelings will net you more information than a bullying and unconcerned approach. That's even true when talking to suspects.)*

118

Ask questions which do not imply answers and which require more than yes or no answers.

**EXAMPLES**

> **Bad:** Was he tall? *(Needs only a yes or no and neither tells you much)*
> **Better:** What was his height?
>
> **Bad:** What kind of weapon did he have? *(Implies that there was a weapon)*
> **Better:** Was there anything in his hands?

Allow people to tell their complete stories once without taking notes. Some people get nervous about you "putting it down in black and white" and might prefer that their statements be "off the record." You also don't want to frustrate them by slowing them down. You can't write as quickly as they speak. After they've blurted out their emotional (rather than factual) and rambling (rather than chronologically ordered) story once, get out your notebook and get the facts you need in the order in which they actually occurred.

Tell them you can't possibly remember all that they said and start writing down (in note style) the important information for your later report. This time go at your pace. Now you'll have the advantage of hearing their story twice. If there are contradictions, note them and ask about them. They may just be emotionally distraught or they may be lying. Either condition tells prosecuting attorneys something about what kind of witnesses they'll be.

Let them do most of the talking. You can't learn much if you are talking all the time. Nothing encourages others to talk more than giving them opportunities to talk.

If your note taking is done at the crime scene itself, you will need to record in addition to the above field notes:

1. Significant **conditions present at the time of your arrival.** *(What did you see, smell and hear when you got there?)*

2. **A chronological account of your actions until you were relieved.** *(What did you do first? second? third?)*

119

3. **Any identification or handling of evidence.** *(Necessary for the "chain of custody" of evidence)*

Public safety reports are used to:

**Record facts into a permanent record.** *(Your report will stay on file forever.)*

**Provide coordination of follow-up activities and investigative leads.** *(Any report of a crime not immediately solved will be forwarded to detectives who will rely on your report to tell them what happened.)*

**Provide the basis for prosecution (and sometimes the defense as well).** *(The processing attorney will decide whether or not to issue a complaint based on what you wrote, not on what you **know** about the case. In most jurisdictions the defense attorney is entitled to a complete copy of your report. A poor report may actually provide the basis of the suspect's defense.)*

**Provide a source for officer evaluation.** *(Supervisors will not always be at your incident scenes. They will know the quality of your work **primarily** by what you write.)*

**Provide statistical data.** *(Need more officers? That need must be established statistically before you will get any new help doing your job. Those statistics come from your reports.)*

**Provide reference material.** *(You will refresh your memory from your report before testifying. Others may even use your report as the basis for lawsuits against others or **you**.)*

The characteristics of good public safety reports are:

**Accuracy** *(Accomplished through noun specificity, past tense, proper punctuation, use of first person, proper use of modifiers.)*

**Conciseness** *(Accomplished through the use of active voice, good word choices.)*

**Clarity** *(Accomplished through the proper use of comparative modifies, subject-verb agreement, pronoun-antecedent agreement, chronological order, proper paragraphing, elimination of jargon/slang except as necessary.)*

**Legibility** *(Accomplished by using only capital letters.)*

**Objectivity** *(Accomplished through the use of facts and inferences, not opinions.)*

**Correct grammar** *(Accomplished through the use of complete and proper sentences.)*

**Correct spelling** *(Accomplished through a lot of memorizing and/or the constant use of a dictionary.)*

**Completeness** *(Accomplished by making sure your report answers these questions: Who? What? Where? When? Why? How?)*

# CHAPTER EIGHT

# THE WELL-WRITTEN REPORT: FROM START TO FINISH

*Reprinted with permission from*
**Criminal Investigation**, Eighth Edition
*by* Wayne W. Bennett and Kären M. Hess
© 2007 Wadsworth/Thomson Learning

Report writing is a skill that takes time and practice to develop. It is *not* a talent—you are not expected to write entertaining literary masterpieces, full of insight and originality. Instead, to write an effective, successful report, you must organize your notes and adhere to some basic standards of written English regarding content and form.

### Organizing Information

A cornerstone of good report writing is organization. Good reports do not just happen. The writer plans in advance in what order the information should be written. Too many officers simply sit down and start writing without giving any thought of how the report should flow, which results in more time spent rewriting and revising later. To use your time most efficiently, first make an informal outline. Next, list what you want to include under each heading in the outline. Review your notes and number each statement to match a heading in your outline. For example, if Section III.C of the outline is headed "description of Suspect #2," write *III.C* in the margin wherever Suspect #2 is described in your notes. List the facts of the investigation in **chronological order** beginning with the response to the call and concluding with the end of the investigation. If the report is long (more than four pages), use headings to guide the reader—for example, "Initial Response," "Crime-Scene Conditions," "Photographs Taken," "Evidence," "Witnesses," "Suspects," and so on. After you complete the outline and determine where each note fits, you are ready to begin writing.

## Structuring the Narrative

Usually the **narrative**, the "story" of the case in chronological order, is structured as follows:

1. The opening paragraph of a police report states the time, date, type of incident, and how you became involved.
2. The next paragraph contains what you were told by the victim or witness. For each person talked to, use a separate paragraph.
3. Next record what you did based on the information you received.
4. The final paragraph states the disposition of the case.

Steps 2 and 3 may be repeated several times in a report on a case where you talk to several witnesses/victims.

## A Brief Look at Law Enforcement Report Forms

While this chapter focuses on writing narrative reports, many departments use box-style law enforcement report forms for certain offenses and incidents. Law enforcement report forms vary greatly in format.

Hess and Wrobleski (p. iv) point out that some report forms "…contain boxes or separate category sections, e.g., property loss section, for placement of descriptive information, addresses and phone numbers of the persons involved. It is unnecessary to repeat this information in the narrative *unless it is needed for clarity* because it tends to interrupt the flow of words and clutter the narrative." In contrast, narrative reports that do *not* use the box-style format include descriptive information, addresses, and phone numbers within the body of the narrative, since no separate section exists for those data.

Read the following excerpt from a narrative report, noting the underlined descriptive information.

> I talked to the victim, Betty Jones, <u>355 Rose ST., Albany, New York, phone 555-9002.</u> Jones told me that her diamond ring was taken during the burglary. The ring was a <u>2-carat diamond stone, platinum setting, with the initials B.A.J. inside the band, valued at $11,500.00.</u>

If these data were, instead, to be formatted into a box-style report, the underlined descriptive information, address, and phone number would be deleted from the narrative *unless that information was needed for clarity*, as shown in the following excerpt:

> The victim, Betty Jones, told me that her diamond ring was taken during the burglary.

Brown and Cox (p. 84) note that formerly many agencies used a three-part report: the blanks at the beginning of the report, a synopsis or summary, and the narrative. They contend that may agencies have moved away from the use of synopses recently. However, if your department does use a synopsis format, include the *who, what, when,* and *where,* but not the *why*: "Concentrate on making the synopsis as brief and clear as possible."

**Characteristics of Effective Reports: Content and Form**

In addition to a well-structured narrative, an effective report exhibits several other characteristics, which generally fall into one of two areas: **content**, or *what* is said, and **form**, or *how* it is written. The effective report writer attends to both content and form, as they are equally important in a well-written report.

The *content* of an effective report is factual, accurate, objective, and complete. The *form* of a well-written report is concise, clear, grammatically and mechanically correct, and written in standard English. An effective report is also organized into paragraphs and written in the past tense, using the first person and active voice. Finally, a well-written report is audience focused, legible, and submitted on time. The table below illustrates the differences between content and form as they relate to investigative reports.

| Content—*what* is said | Form—*how* it is said |
|---|---|
| The elements of the crime | Word choice |
| Descriptions of suspects, victims, etc. | Sentence and paragraph length |
| Evidence collected | Spelling |
| Actions of victim, witnesses, suspects | Punctuation |
| Observations: weather, road conditions, smells, sounds oddities, etc. | Grammar |
| | Mechanics |

## Factual

The basic purpose of any investigation report is to record the facts. A **fact** is a statement that can be proven. (It may be proven false, but it is still classified as a factual statement.) The truthfulness or accuracy of facts will be discussed shortly. First consider how to clearly distinguish among three basic types of statements.

> Fact: A statement that can be proven.
>> *Example*: The man has a bulge in his black leather jacket pocket.
> Inference: A conclusion based on reasoning.
>> *Example:* The man is probably carrying a gun.
> Opinion: A personal belief.
>> *Example:* Black leather jackets are cool.

A well-written report is factual. It does *not* contain opinions. You can discuss and debate facts and inferences logically and reasonably and come to some agreement on them. An **opinion**, however, reflects personal beliefs, on which there is seldom agreement. For example, how do you resolve the differences between two people arguing over whether pie tastes better than cake? You can't. It's simply a matter of personal preference.

Inferences (conclusions) can prove valuable in a report, provided they are based on sufficient evidence. Sometimes it is hard to distinguish between facts and inferences. One way to tell them apart is to ask the question "Can the statement be simply proven true or false, or do I need other facts to make it reasonable?" For example, if you wanted to verify the statement "The driver of the truck was drunk," you would need to supply several facts to support your inference. One such fact might be that he had a blood alcohol content over .10. Other facts might include your observations, such as his slurred speech, his red and watery eyes, five empty beer cans behind the driver's seat, and the strong odor of an alcoholic beverage on the driver's breath.

An **inference** is not really true or false; it is sound or unsound (believable or not believable). And the only way to make an inference sound (believable) is to provide facts to support it. One way to ensure that your inference is clearly an inference, instead of a fact, would be to use the word *apparently* or *appeared* (e.g., "The driver appeared to be under the influence of alcohol").

Inferences are also referred to as **conclusionary language**. Avoid conclusionary language by *showing*, not *telling*. For example, do not write, "The man *could not* walk in a straight line." You do not know what another person can or cannot do. A more factual way to report this would be "The man *did* not walk a straight line." Even better would be "The man stepped 18 inches to the right of the line twice and 12 inches to the left of the line three times." Consider this account by Rutledge (pp. 110-111):

> I once got into a drunk driving trial where, according to the arresting officer, the defendant had "repeatedly refused" to take a chemical test. The defendant was named Sanchez, and at trial he insisted, through a court interpreter, that he neither spoke nor understood any English. His defense that he couldn't possibly refuse an English-language request when he couldn't even understand it sold well with the jury, especially after the officer had to admit that he didn't recall exactly how or in what specific words the defendant had "refused" a test. The cop couldn't live with his conclusionary report. Neither could I. The defendant lived with it very comfortably, and he owed his acquittal directly to the same officer who had arrested him. Ironic?
>
> We would have been much better off if the cop had never used the conclusionary word "refused," but had instead married the defendant to his own words! The report could have helped the prosecution, instead of the defense, if it had been written like this:
>
> *After I explained the need to take a chemical test, Sanchez said, in Spanish-accented English, "Screw you, cop...I ain't taking no test, man. Why don't you take it yourself?" I told him he had to take a test or his license would be suspended. He said, "I don't need no license to drive, man. I know lots of people drive without a license. You ain't scared me, man, and I ain't taking no stupid test. I'll beat this thing."*
>
> See the difference? Not a single conclusion or interpretation. The reader gets to "hear" the same things the writer heard. The officer could have lived with something like that—the defendant couldn't.

The following conclusionary statements can also jeopardize the effectiveness and value of investigative reports:

- "They denied any involvement in the crime."

- "She confessed to seven more arsons."
- "He admitted breaking into the warehouse."
- "He consented to a search of the trunk."
- "She waived her rights per Miranda."

The following table presents alternatives to conclusionary words and phrases that will make reports more factual and, thus, more effective and valuable

| You Can't Live with These | So Use | You Can't Live with These | So Use |
|---|---|---|---|
| Indicated, refused, admitted, confessed, denied, consented, identified, waived, profanity, threatening, obscene, evasive, deceptive | A verbatim or approximate quotation of what was said | Angry, upset, nervous, excited, happy, unhappy, intentional, accidental, heard, saw, knew, thought | The source of your conclusions (when you're attributing them to someone else) |
| Assaulted, attacked, accosted, confrontation, escalated, struggle ensued, resisted, battered, intimidated, bullied, forced | A factual account of who did what | Matching the description, suspicious, furtive, strange, abnormal, typical, uncooperative, belligerent, combative, obnoxious, abusive, exigent | The reasons for your belief that these apply |

Conclusionary language may also lead to inaccuracies in your report.

**Accurate**

To be useful, facts must be accurate. An effective report accurately records the correct time and date, correct names of all persons involved, correct phone numbers and addresses, and exact descriptions of the crime scene, property, vehicles, and suspects involved. Have people spell their names. Repeat spellings and numbers for verification. Recheck measurements. Be sure of the accuracy of your facts. An inaccurately recorded license number may result in losing a witness or suspect. Inaccurate measurement or recording of the distance and location of skid marks, bullet holes, or bodies may lead to wrong conclusions.

To be accurate, you must be specific. For example, it is better to say, "The car was traveling in excess of 90 mph" than to say, "The car was traveling fast." It is more accurate to describe a suspect as "approximately six-foot-six" than to describe him as "tall."

You must have the facts in the case correct. If your report says four men were involved in a robbery and in reality, three men and a woman were involved, your report would be inaccurate. If you are unsure of the gender of the individuals involved in an incident, identify them as "people," "suspects," "witnesses," or whatever the case may be. If your facts come from the statement of a witness rather than from your own observation, say so in your report.

Phrases such as "He saw what happened" or "He heard what happened" are conclusionary and may also lead to inaccuracies in your report. People can be looking directly at something and not see it, either because they are simply not paying attention or because they have terrible vision. The same is true of hearing. Again, you do not know what another person sees or hears. Your report should say, "He *said* he saw what happened" or "He looked directly at the man committing the crime."

Another common conclusionary statement found in police reports is, "The check was signed by John Doe." Unless you saw John Doe sign the check, the correct (accurate) statement would be, "The check was signed John Doe." The little two-letter word *by* can create tremendous problems for you on the witness stand.

Vague, imprecise words have no place in police reports. The following words and phrases should *not* be used because they are not specific: *a few, several, many, frequently, often.* Finally, instead of writing *contacted,* be specific by using *telephoned, visited, e-mailed,* or whatever particular mode of communication was involved.

## Objective

You have seen that reports must be factual. It is possible, however, to include only factual statements in a report and still not be objective. Being **objective** means being nonopinionated, fair, and impartial. Lack of objectivity can result from either of two things: poor word choice or omission of facts.

Word choice is an often overlooked—yet very important—aspect of report writing. Consider, for example, the difference in effect achieved by these three sentences:

> The man cried.
> The man wept.
> The man blubbered.

Although you want to be specific, you must also be aware of the effect of the words you use. Words that have little emotional effect, e.g., *cried*, are called **denotative** words. The denotative meaning of a word is its *objective* meaning. In contrast, words that do have an emotional effect are called **connotative** words, e.g., *wept, blubbered*. The connotative meaning of a word comprises its positive or negative overtones. In the three sentences above, only the first sentence is truly objective. The second sentence makes the reader feel sympathetic toward the man. The third makes the reader unsympathetic.

Likewise, derogatory, biased terms referring to a person's race, ethnicity, religion, or sexual preference have no place in police reports. A defense attorney will certainly capitalize on words with emotional overtones and attempt to show bias. Even the use of *claimed* rather than *stated* can be used to advantage by a defense attorney, who might suggest that the officer's use of *claimed* implies that the officer did not believe the statement.

Also, use the correct word. Do not confuse words that are similar, or you can be made to appear ridiculous. For example, this sentence in an officer's report would probably cast suspicion on the officer's intelligence: "During our training we spent four hours learning to resemble a firearm and the remainder of the time learning defective driving."

Keep to the facts. Include all facts, even those that may appear to be damaging to your case. Objectivity is attained by including both sides of the account. **Slanting,** that is, including only one side of a story or only facts that tend to prove or support the officer's theory, can also make a report nonobjective. A good report includes both sides of an incident when possible. Even when facts tend to go against your theory about what happened, you are obligated to include them. Omitting important facts is *not* objective.

## Complete

Information kept in the reporting officer's head is of no value to anyone else involved in the case. An effective report contains answers to at least six basic questions: Who? What? When? Where? How? and Why? The *who, what, when,* and *where* questions should be answered by factual statements. The *how* and *why* statements may require inferences. When this is the case, clearly label the statements as inferences. This is especially true when answering the question of cause. To avoid slanting the report, record all possible causes no matter how implausible they may seem at the time.

If a form is used for your reports, all applicable blanks at the top of the form should be filled in. Certain agencies require a slash mark, the abbreviation NA (not applicable), or the abbreviation UNK (unknown) to be placed in any box that does not contain information.

Each specific type of crime requires different information.

## Concise

Being **concise** means making every word count without leaving out important facts. Avoid wordiness; length alone does not ensure quality. Some reports can be written in half a page; others require 12 or even 20 pages. No specific length can be prescribed, but strive to include all relevant information in as few words as possible.

You can reduce wordiness in two basic ways: (1) Leave out unnecessary information and (2) use as few words as possible to record the necessary facts. For example, do not write, "The car was blue in color"; write "The car was blue." A phrase such as "information which is of a confidential nature" should be recognized as a wordy way of saying "confidential information."

Do not make the mistake of equating conciseness with brevity. Being brief is not the same as being concise. For example, compare:

Brief:    She drove a car.
Concise: She drove a maroon 1992 Chevrolet Caprice.
Wordy:   She drove a car that was a 1992 Chevrolet Caprice and was maroon in color.

Avoiding wordiness does not mean eliminating details; it means eliminating empty words and phrases. Consider these examples of how to make wordy phrases more concise:

| Wordy | Concise |
|---|---|
| made note of the fact that | noted |
| square in shape | square |
| in the amount of | for |
| despite the fact that | although |
| for the purpose of determining | to determine |

**Clear**

An investigation report should have only one interpretation. Two people should be able to read the report and come up with the same word-picture and understanding of the events. Make certain your sentences can be read only one way. For example, consider the following unclear sentences:

- When completely plastered, officers who volunteer will paint the locker room.
- Miami police kill a man with a machete.
- Three cars were reported stolen by the Los Angeles police yesterday.
- Police begin campaign to run down jaywalkers.
- Squad helps dog bite victim.

Rewrite such sentences so that only one interpretation is possible. For example, the first sentence in the previous list might read: "Officers who volunteer will paint the locker room after it is completely plastered." The third sentence might read: "According to the Los Angeles police, three cars were reported stolen yesterday."

Follow these guidelines to make your reports clearer:

- *Use specific, concrete facts and details.* Compare the following statements and determine which is clearer:

    1. The car sped away and turned the corner.
    2. The gold 1996 Cadillac Fleetwood pulled away from the curb, accelerated to approximately 65 mph, and then turned off First Street onto Brooklyn Boulevard.

The second statement is clearer because it contains concrete facts and details.

- *Keep descriptive words and phrases as close as possible to the words they describe.* Compare the following statements and determine which is clearer.

    1. He replaced the gun into the holster which he had just fired.
    2. He replaced the gun, which he had just fired, into the holster.

The second statement is clearer because the phrase "which he had just fired" is placed close to the word it modifies (*gun*).

- *Use diagrams and sketches when a description is complex.* This is especially true in reports of crashes, homicides, and burglaries. The diagrams do not have to be artistic masterpieces. They should, however, be in approximate proportion and should help the reader follow the narrative portion of the report.

- *Do not use uncommon abbreviations.* Some abbreviations (such as *Mr., Dr., Ave., St., Feb., Aug., NY, CA*) are so commonly used that they require no explanation. Other abbreviations, however, are commonly used only in law enforcement. Do not use these in your reports, since not all readers will understand them. Confusion can result if two people have different interpretations of an abbreviation. For example, what does S.O.B. mean to you? To most people it has a negative meaning. But for people in the health field, it means "short of breath." Meier and

133

Adams (p. 102) provide this example as something that can be used in your notes but should not appear, as such , in a report:

Unk / B / M / , nfd, driving unk / Chry / 4DBlu, nfd

Instead, write out:

Unknown black male (no further description available) was seen driving a blue Chrysler 4-door (no further description available).

Use only abbreviations common to everyone.

- *Use short sentences, well organized into short paragraphs.*
  Short sentences are easier to read. Likewise, paragraphs should be relatively short, usually five to ten sentences. Each question to be answered in the report should have its own paragraph. The report should be organized logically. Most commonly it begins with *when* and *where* and then tells *who* and *what*. The *what* should be in chronological order—that is, going from beginning to end without skipping back and forth.

### Grammatically and Mechanically Correct

If you were to *hear* the words "Your chances of being promoted are good if you can write effective reports," you would probably feel differently than if you were to *read* the same words written like this: "yur chanses of bein promottid are gud. if you kin rite afectiv riports." The **mechanics**— spelling, capitalization, and punctuation—involved in translating ideas and spoken words into written words are important. Yet, as Clark (p. 56) observes: "Probably the most common writing error police officers make is misspelled words." Mistakes in spelling, punctuation, capitalization, and grammar give the impression that the writer is careless, uneducated, or stupid—maybe all three!

Use a dictionary and a grammar book if in doubt about how to write something. The dictionary can tell you not only how to spell a word but also whether it should be capitalized and how it should be abbreviated. To make spelling less difficult, consider using a *speller/divider*. These little reference books contain thousands of the most commonly used words, showing their spelling and how they are divided. The reader is not distracted by definitions, information on the history of the word, synonyms, and so on. The most important advantage is that one speller/divider page has as many words on it as 15 to 20 dictionary pages.

Use caution when relying on grammar- and spell-checker programs to find mistakes in computerized documents. Sievert (p. 37) observes:

> In what is probably the ultimate irony, one of the solutions to improved report writing is also one of the causes of imprecise writing. Studies indicate word processor Grammar Check functions will catch about 60% of the errors. This is a benefit to the average writer, yet reliance on Grammar Check reduces the skill set of the writer and leaves almost half the errors unflagged. Even worse, the Spell Checker provides an accurate spelling, but it does not check meaning—resulting, at times, in the grotesque misuse of a word.

For an example, if an investigator wrote that a victim of an assault was unable to be interviewed because "she had lapsed into a *comma*," or that a suspect had been restrained because "he was acting *erotically*," when what the writer meant to say was "coma" and "erratically," respectively, the reader might question the investigator's intelligence and/or attention to detail.

## Written in Standard English

People often disagree about what standard English is. And the standards between spoken and written English differ. For example, if you were to *say*, "I'm gonna go walkin' in the mornin'," it would probably sound all right. People often drop the "g" when they speak. In writing, however, this is not acceptable.

Just as there are rules for spelling, capitalization, and punctuation, there are rules for *what* words are used *when*. For example, it is standard to say "he doesn't" rather than "he don't"; "I don't have any" rather than "I ain't got none"; "he and I are partners" rather than "him and me are partners."

Your experience with English will often tell you what is standard and what is not—especially if you have lived in surroundings in which standard

135

English is used. If you speak standard English, you will probably also write in standard English. But that is not always true.

## Paragraphs

As discussed earlier, in structuring the narrative and making your report clear, effective writers use paragraphs to guide the reader. Keep the paragraphs short (usually 100 words or less). Skip a line to indicate the beginning of a new paragraph. Discuss only one subject in each paragraph. Start a new paragraph when you change speakers, locations, time or ideas— for example, when you go from observations to descriptions to statements.

Paragraphs are reader friendly, guiding the reader through your report. Most paragraphs should be 5 to 6 sentences, although they may be a single sentence or up to 10 or 15 sentences on occasion.

## Past Tense

Write in the **past tense** throughout the report. Past-tense writing uses verbs that show that events have already occurred. Your report contains what *was* true at the time you took your notes. Use of present tense can cause tremendous problems later. For example, suppose you wrote, "John Doe *lives* at 100 South Street and *works* for Ace Trucking Company." One year later you find yourself on the witness stand with a defense attorney asking you: "Now, Officer, your report says that John Doe lives at 100 South Street. Is that correct?" You may not know, and you would have to say so. The next question: "Now, Officer, your report says John Doe works for Ace Trucking Company. Is *that* correct?" Again, you may be uncertain and be forced into an "I don't know" response. Use of the past tense in your report avoids this problem.

## First Person

Use the first person to refer to yourself. **First person** in English uses the words *I, me, my, we, us,* and *our.* The sentence "*I* responded to the call" is written in the first person. This is in contrast to "*This officer* responded to the call," which uses the third person. Whether you remember your English classes and discussions of first-, second-, and third-person singular and plural is irrelevant. Simply remember to refer to yourself as *I* rather than as *this officer.*

## Active Voice

A sentence may be either active or passive. This is an easy distinction to make if you think about what the words *active* and *passive* mean. (Forget about the term *voice*; it is a technical grammatical term you do not need to understand to write well.) In the **active voice** the subject of the sentence performs the actions—for example, "I wrote the report." This is in contrast to the *passive* voice, in which the subject does nothing—for example, "The report was written by me." The report did not do anything. The problem with the passive voice is that often the *by* is left off—for example, "The report was written." Later, no one knows who did the writing. Passive voice results in a "whodunit" that can have serious consequences in court.

Statements are usually clearer in active voice. Although most sentences should be in the active voice, a *passive* sentence is acceptable in the following situations:

1. If the doer of the action is unknown, unimportant, or obvious.

*Example*: The gun had been fired three times.

We don't know who fired it. This is better than "Someone had fired the gun three times."

*Example:* The woman has been arrested four times.

Who arrested her each time is not important.

*Example*: Felix Umburger was paroled in April.

*Who* is obviously the parole board.

2. When you want to call special attention to the receiver of the action rather than the doer.

*Example:* Officer Morris was promoted after the examination.

Not only is it unimportant who promoted him, you want to call attention to Officer Morris.

3.  When it would be unfair or embarrassing to be mentioned by name.

*Example*: The program was postponed because the wrong film was sent.

*Better than:* The program was postponed because Sergeant Fairchild sent the wrong film.

*Example*: Insufficient evidence was gathered at the crime scene.

*Better than:* Investigator Hanks gathered insufficient evidence at the crime scene.

## Audience Focused

Always consider who your audience is. Police reports have a diversity of possible readers. Given these varied backgrounds and individuals with limited familiarity with law enforcement terminology, the necessity for audience-focused reports becomes obvious. By keeping in mind this diverse audience, you will construct a report that is reader friendly.

One way to be reader friendly is to be certain that the narrative portion of your report can stand alone. That calls for eliminating such phrases as *the above*. A reader-friendly report does not begin, "On the above date at the above time, I responded to the above address to investigate a burglary in progress."

Using such phrases presents two problems. First, if readers take time to look "above" to find the information, their train of thought is broken. It is difficult to find where to resume reading, and time is wasted. Second, if readers do *not* take time to look "above," important information is not conveyed, and it is very likely that the reader, perhaps subconsciously, will be wondering what would have been found "above." If information is important enough to refer to in your report, include it in the narrative. Do not take the lazy approach and ask your reader to search for the information "above."

Another way to write a reader-friendly report is to steer clear of police lingo and other bureaucratic language and use plain English. Meier and Adams (p. 99) point out that officers tend to speak and write in a dialect of English they call "Cop Speak," which the majority of the public often does not understand. In explaining why investigators and other law enforcement officers should avoid jargon and other "insider" terminology when communicating with those outside the field, Moore (p. 266) notes: "This type of language makes it seem as if you don't share the same language as the public you serve. It goes against the basic principles of community policing and sets criminal justice agencies and their personnel apart from the very people they rely on for information, funding and authority."

**Legible and On Time**

It does little good to learn to write well if no one can read it or if the report is turned in after it was needed. Ideally, reports should be typed; and in today's computer-driven world, most reports are generated this way. Sometimes, however, this is not practical or possible. In fact, a poorly typed report is often as difficult to read as an illegible one. If you do not type your reports, and if you know that you have poor handwriting, you may want to print your reports by hand. Granted, this is slower than cursive, but a report that cannot be read is of little use to anyone. Whether your reports are typed, written, or printed, make certain that others can read them easily and that they are submitted on time.

# PART V

# *INTERROGATION AND TESTIFYING IN COURT*

# CHAPTER NINE

# ETHICAL CONSIDERATIONS IN INTERVIEWS AND INTERROGATIONS

The goal of criminal investigation is to successfully identify the offender so that the appropriate action can be taken. It is for this reason many investigators become overzealous in their quest for the "truth" while forfeiting their ethical responsibilities. A successful investigation does not always mean the identity of the offender is determined. An investigation can be successful while it remains unsolved. In many text, successful investigations are defined as those in which all logical investigative leads are developed and completed. Not all investigations can or will be solved. In many cases the best that can be done is to conduct a thorough and timely investigation with the knowledge that all that could be done was accomplished, and that insufficient information existed to provide a solved investigation. Why, then, do investigators forfeit their ethics during their investigations? Why would an interviewer risk the outcome of an investigation or the prosecution of an offender? There must be answers to these questions since investigations are compromised on a regular basis. This chapter will look at the various reasons investigators compromise their investigations during the interview and interrogation processes.

### The Need for Ethics

Ethical standards must always be maintained. During the past few decades, law enforcement has been subjected to detailed scrutiny. Crime scene investigators have been interrogated in court about their procedures, detectives about their decisions, and patrol officers about their interactions with the public. Recent years have seen the video camera introduced as an objective lens upon law enforcement. Officers now feel that their behavior and mere presence could easily wind up on the evening news. Officers have been indicted, tried, and convicted for physically abusive behavior. All the textbooks, academies, and in-service training sessions in the world will not remedy this situation until law enforcement personnel take a personal interest in sharpening their ethics.

There will be a number of situations in which interviewers will be tempted to solve a case through the use of unlawful inducement or unacceptable tactics. There are many techniques available to the interviewer with which to gain information. The law provides remedies for illegally obtained information. Information gathered from suspects through unacceptable means will be held as inadmissible in court. Some questions then arise. Had the interviewer used ethical tactics during the interrogation, would the courts have allowed the information into court, thus securing a conviction? Was there an alternate technique available to the interviewer? What actions are to be taken with the stubborn suspect? It is believed that *everyone* will confess given the right motivation to do so. This statement should be rephrased stating that everyone will confess given the right *ethical* motivation to do so. The difficulty here is the suspect does not have to follow any rules, but the interviewer does. The suspect is expected to lie and do whatever is necessary to avoid detection and punishment. This uneven battleground does provide the interviewer with some legal recourse. For example, in the United Kingdom it is considered unethical and illegal for the police to lie to suspects during their interrogations. The rationale is that the investigation must have a high ethical standard, and if done correctly, lies would not be necessary during the investigation. Likewise, certain investigative techniques are considered illegal in Korea.

### Real-Life Scenario:
*During a blackmarketing investigation, an American military investigator conducted a "sting" operation to identify and apprehend a Korean blackmarketeer. Upon catching the suspect, the Korean police threatened to arrest the American investigator, stating that it was illegal to commit a crime to catch a criminal.*

Of course, in the United States, undercover or sting operations are commonplace as long as certain legal guidelines are followed. Lying to suspects during an interrogation is also considered ethical, within certain boundaries.

## When, How, and Why to Lie

The old adage "honesty is the best policy" is often the best advice anyone can follow. Whenever someone is identified as a liar, anything they say from that point on is considered suspect. This will hold true with the interviewer as well. When an investigation results in ample evidence against a suspect it is unadvisable to lie during the interrogation. The suspect, if responsible for the crime, usually knows more about the situation than anyone. The suspect constantly evaluates the information provided by the interviewer. Once the suspect believes the interviewer is relying upon lies as "facts of the case," the suspect wins with the knowledge that further lying will help prevent his discovery. Lying should never be used as a routine interrogation technique. Knowing when to lie and what to lie about will help the interviewer gain powerful confessions. The decision to lie to a suspect remains with the interrogator, and should only be considered in light of the interrogation's progress. When an investigation falls short of sufficient evidence against a suspect, lies may help in convincing the suspect that all is lost and that by confessing, he would only help his legal situation. How to convince a suspect of this is an important factor.

## Making Deals

Since many suspects are interested in making a deal, it is easy to understand why this type of tactic would produce an admission or confession. Unless provided with such powers by legal authorities, such as the district attorney, interviewers cannot lie to suspects concerning such outcomes. By telling a suspect that a deal can be reached based upon his confession, the interviewer is attempting to deliver something beyond his reach. It is true that prosecutorial deals can be reached based upon confessions of guilt, however the official making this offer must possess the legal authority to do so. Rather than offering a deal to the suspect, interviewers can state that they will testify at trial for the suspect based upon his cooperation. This offer is easily lived up to. Not only will the suspect receive his end of the bargain, but the interviewer establishes his credibility as well. The interviewer has not lied about what his actions will be.

**Real-Life Scenario:**
*The author arrested a man for selling cocaine. During the interrogation the offender refused to admit to selling drugs of any kind. Shortly before trial the suspect contacted the author wanting to supply information in*

145

*return for a prosecutorial deal. The author offered to testify at trial as to the suspect's cooperativeness if any successful drug investigations resulted from his information. The suspect provided information producing numerous drug related arrests. The author then testified that the suspect was cooperative and instrumental in identifying various drug dealers in the community. The suspect was found guilty, and sentenced to imprisonment. The judge commented that his cooperativeness was self-serving and did not negate the seriousness of his offense. However, the author's integrity was maintained.*

### Only Good Can Come From This

Similar to lying about prosecutorial deals, it is also unethical to tell a suspect that only good can come from his confession. Many suspects injure their family members physically or emotionally. Their confession will no doubt cause a breakup within the family. The suspect will be imprisoned; the family will alienate the suspect, and the family unit as a whole will be destroyed. How can an interviewer tell a suspect that only good things will result from his confession? The suspect's later claim of unlawful influence may be upheld as unlawful coercion if he was convinced that a confession would prevent damage to his family. Rather than telling the suspect that his confession and cooperation would help the family situation, offering professional help would be more realistic and ethical. Many offenders recognize the need for professional mental health or family counseling. The corrections system of the United States does offer these rehabilitative services to its population. Like many people with personal problems, such as alcohol or drugs, they can only be successfully treated or "cured" if they recognize that they have the problem and willingly accept professional help.

**Real-Life Scenario:**
*A sexual offender was arrested for sexually molesting his teenage daughter. The offender was visibly distraught over the impending imprisonment, loss of his job, and the damage to his family. The author, rather than convincing the suspect that his confession would ultimately help his family, advised the suspect to accept the consequences of his behavior thus seeking the professional mental help the system had to offer. No predictions of repairing the damage to his family or preventing incarceration were made. The suspect opted to cooperate with the author and provided a detailed confession as to his actions. The suspect, working through legal counsel,*

*did obtain professional help prior to trial. His efforts were noted by the courts at sentencing, whereby he was sentenced to three years of probation.*

The ethical question now arises: is it the responsibility of the interviewer to assist the offender in preventing due punishment as depicted in the above case? Or is it the interviewer's only responsibility to obtain a confession so that the criminal justice system can take its course no matter what the outcome? Clearly, interviewers are not bound by any regulation or ethical canon to arrange or assist offenders in receiving professional guidance for their futures. However, if the interview is to be completed successfully and ethically, interviewers must consider the desired outcome of a confession rather than punishment. It is debatable whether the author prevented incarceration in the above case. The primary goal of the interview was to obtain a confession so that the investigation could be continued and successfully resolved. It was possible that the suspect's legal counsel would have sought professional help for his client in any event, thus obtaining probation for his client.

### Violating Privileged Communications

Suspects possess what is known as privileged communications. A privileged communication is an exchange of information between the suspect and a person identified by law as having strict confidentiality. The most common privileged communications are between the suspect and clergy, attorney, and spouse.

### Posing as Clergy

The law respects the relationship between clergy and penitent so much so, that suspects can confess to crimes without the fear that the clergyman will repeat the information to the authorities. If clergy were made to provide this information to the authorities, it would cause irreparable damage to the religious institutions of this country. As seen during State of California v. Simpson, the discussion held between Rosie Grier and Orenthal Simpson was protected, even though Simpson clearly revealed information to a third party not governed by the privileged communication process. Whenever a suspect declares information before a third party not recognized as part of the privileged communication, the third party can testify concerning the statement as an exception to hearsay.

**Real-Life Scenario:**

*The court judge promised Simpson that he would have a private discussion with Grier, a recognized clergy. A detention deputy was seated in a small glass-enclosed booth watching the meeting. During the discussion, Simpson became angry and yelled out information that was deemed by the prosecution as an exception to hearsay. The prosecution attempted to have this statement entered into trial as evidence against Simpson. The state argued that since Simpson knew the deputy was in the booth and yelled out loudly enough anyway, he forfeited his protection of the privileged communication. The trial judge opined that since he promised Simpson privacy, he would exclude the statement from trial. Grier could not be compelled to repeat any statements made by Simpson.*

Many have reviewed and commented on the judge's opinion. The state argued that the court met its promise of a private meeting between Simpson and Grier, and that Simpson voluntarily provided information to the deputy by his own actions. The judge, unrelenting in his opinion, stated that his promise to Simpson was to be upheld.

Religion has its place in the interrogation. However, any interrogator who poses as a cleric for the express purpose of obtaining a confession from a suspect would be unethical in his behavior. Suspects would expect that any information they provide to the "cleric" would be private in nature and not provided to the courts to be used against them. Any information obtained from the suspect would clearly be inadmissible at trial. Interrogators can, however, pray along with suspects and discuss religion in a general sense. At no time may an interrogator give the suspect the notion that his statement is equal to that of a religious confession.

**Posing as an Attorney**

One of the most obvious privileged communications is that of attorney and client. Even though many clients refuse to tell their attorneys everything about their involvement in crimes, their communications are protected for the benefit of the client regardless of guilt or innocence. Again, it would be grossly unethical for an interrogator to pose as an attorney in order to solicit a confession. Many first-time suspects ask their interviewers for legal advice during the rights advisal phase of the interview. Suspects routinely ask questions like "Do I need a lawyer?" or "What should I do?" The proper response from the interviewer is to advise the suspect to make their best decision without any prompting from the interviewer. The interviewer may assist the subject in making this decision, however, by stating that a lawyer can be obtained at any time. In many instances, a review of the suspect's rights will help the suspect decide on what course of action to take.

**Real-Life Scenario:**
*While conducting an interrogation, the author advised a suspect of his rights against self-incrimination. When asked if he wanted a lawyer, the suspect stated that he thought the author was a lawyer due to his manner of dress, even though proper identification was provided at the beginning of the interview. The author then clarified his position as an investigator. Had the author ignored the suspect's belief that he was a lawyer, any subsequent confession would have been clearly inadmissible. Knowingly allowing a suspect to believe the interviewer to be a lawyer would be unethical conduct.*

**Promises**

Interviewers are not in the position to make promises to suspects in return for confessions. The likelihood that the courts will recognize and uphold a promise made by an interviewer is slight. It is entirely possible, depending on what the promise is, that the court will find that unlawful coercion was used against the suspect, making the admission or confession inadmissible. Can a prosecutorial deal be regarded as a promise? In light of the authority held by the prosecutor, an offer or promise of immunity is considered legal and not coercive since information from the suspect will not be used against him in court. If an interviewer makes a promise against prosecution to a suspect in return for possibly incriminating information, then what is gained is clearly inadmissible. In some instances, minor offenses can be deemed insignificant as compared to other offenses. Interviewers may want to forfeit the lesser offense against the suspect in return for identifying an offender in a different investigation. It is always advisable to coordinate such efforts with the prosecutor before promising or even suggesting protection against prosecution.

**Chapter Summary**

Interrogators must consider the ramifications of unethical conduct. Any indication of unlawfully coercive questioning will not only destroy hours of investigative work, but could damage the reputation of the interrogator. Lies told to the suspect must be founded upon ethics and legal responsibility. Obvious lies will only convince the suspect that the interrogator is lacking sufficient information to prove his guilt. Only proper legal authorities can offer suspects prosecutorial deals. Any interrogator who offers such a deal in return for a confession is practicing unethical behavior. This will result in an inadmissible confession. Interrogators can offer to testify in court as to the cooperativeness of the suspect, if desired. Predicting outcomes, whether they are prosecutorial or personal, is beyond the ability of the interrogator. By predicting what will happen, the interrogator risks unlawfully coercing the suspect to confess. Posing as clergy or a lawyer will terribly mislead the suspect into confessing. Suspects enjoy the right of privileged communications in these areas.

# CHAPTER TEN

# INTERVIEWING AND
# INTERROGATION: TECHNIQUES

The term "interrogation" suggests an adversarial meeting, where one person is the questioner and the other person provides the answers. Unlike the witness interview, which is a two-way conversation with a common goal, the interrogator controls the interrogation. This results in a one-way conversation with opposing goals, those being the truth for the interrogator, and deception for the suspect. How the truth is obtained and who wins the battle of the minds is the essence of all interrogations. The interrogator is merely asking the suspect to confess to his actions, however serious, so that the information can be provided to the courts for the purposes of conviction and punishment. Beyond this, the suspect must want to do this willingly and voluntarily. That is a lot to ask of a person, especially when they know they are guilty of the offense under investigation. Since many suspects have confessed their crimes, it is a wonder why they agreed to talk in the first place. Was it the approach of the interrogator? Did the suspects attempt to beat the system by "acting honest"? These issues are explored below.

## Techniques

The following is a discussion of commonly used interrogative techniques. Upon reviewing this list and their methods, it will be noted that many of them can be used in conjunction with one another. In fact, many interrogators actually invent their own techniques based upon these. It is recommended that the student interrogator select the techniques that are most comfortable and successful for them, and further develop them.

## How Investigations Work

Perhaps the best interrogation technique to discuss first is the explanation of how investigations work. If a suspect can be convinced of the invariable success of the investigation itself, then the probability of obtaining a confession increases significantly. Many people, including the suspect, have no idea how investigations are conducted. Explaining the investigative process to the suspect will affirm in his mind that evidence will be found, no matter how good he believed his attempts to prevent discovery were. This technique can be used in any interrogation , and with any suspect, since all crimes involve an investigative process. For example, a rape investigation has several parts to it. Each part is significant in its evidence. The following explanation can be provided to a suspect to reinforce the success of the investigation:

"A rape investigation produces an abundance of evidence. First, there are three separate crime scenes. The physical location of the incident will produce evidence concerning what happened and who was involved. Whenever someone commits a crime they will leave behind evidence of their presence. They will leave behind fingerprints, body fluids, hairs, fibers, or other minute particles that can be used to establish someone's identity. The victim and suspect's bodies are also separate crime scenes. The suspect in a rape will make bodily contact with the victim. Therefore, body fluids will be exchanged. Their clothing will transfer hair or fibers. By taking evidence from all three scenes, the physical location, the victim's body and clothing, and the suspect's body and clothing, there will be enough physical evidence to prove who committed the crime. Fingerprints can positively identify a suspect, DNA can identify a suspect beyond probability, hairs and fibers can provide information as to where the incident occurred. Beyond the physical evidence, there will be the victim's statement, as well as witness observations. The amount of evidence can be overwhelming. How can anyone deny involvement in the face of such evidence?

The suspect will soon understand that continued denials will be fruitless, since forensic science and investigative techniques will make escape virtually impossible. The interrogator can then ask the suspect to provide his own opinion regarding the probability that the responsible person will be identified. No doubt the suspect will agree that enough evidence will be

152

available to make the proper identification. This is a strong start for the interrogation, since the appropriate mind-set has occurred.

## Mistakes

We all make mistakes. This is a very believable statement. The rationalization in this technique is clear; the suspect made a mistake and did not mean to commit the crime under investigation. It is reasonable to state that a suspect may have mistaken the identity of the victim. Stealing property could be explained by claiming that a mistake was made in the ownership of the item. If the interrogator can "explain away" the crime, the suspect will most likely want to take the "out" offered him. The legal question of "mistake of fact" is for the courts to decide and not the interrogator. The logic in this technique is for the suspect to desire the courts to listen and decide in his favor. However, this can only occur if the suspect will admit to making the mistake in the first place!

## Lies

As interrogators, we would like the suspect to be truthful, and to provide a confession about what occurred. We do know that suspects often lie about almost anything as long as it saves them from punishment. The courts have held that lying to a suspect during an interrogation is a legal strategy as long as it is not based upon unlawful coercion. We cannot lie to a suspect telling him that confessing would prevent his prosecution, or that certain punishment would not occur. Lying is not unlawfully coercive since the suspect had the option of not agreeing to the interrogation in the first place. Is lying to a suspect a good strategy? This depends on what the lie is. Anytime a lie is told to a suspect during interrogation, the interrogator should be sure the suspect doesn't catch him being deceptive. If this happens, the credibility of the investigator is severely damaged, and the possibility of a confession lessens significantly. For example, telling a suspect that his fingerprints were found at the crime scene seems like pretty strong evidence. Wouldn't such strong evidence convince a suspect to admit to a crime or at least to being present? If the suspect wore gloves and knew that he was careful enough not to leave fingerprints, then the suspect wins with the knowledge that the interrogator has no real evidence against him. If the interrogator did have evidence, he would have presented it. Lies that are told to the suspect are lies that cannot be refuted by the suspect. The suspect must either accept the interrogator's version of the

153

information, or continue to deny regardless of what is said. In either case, the subject cannot doubt the interrogator. Lies should be simple and believable.

### Real-Life Scenario:
*Three men were suspected of committing a burglary. The majority of the evidence pointed to one of the men in particular. The other two suspects left the area and were no longer available. The third suspect was intentionally interviewed after they left. The author, after confirming that the suspect was aware that his friends had departed the area, told the suspect that they had supplied information naming him as the person responsible for the burglary. The suspect was also told that the interview was postponed until the two men left. The suspect then confessed to the crime since he felt that his friends had betrayed him, thus guaranteeing their elimination as suspects.*

There are two points to observe in this instance. First, the suspect could not refute the information presented by the interrogator. Second, the suspect knew that the interrogator was being truthful when he reported that the other two suspects left the area. This convinced the suspect that the interrogator was being honest, and that he possessed sufficient evidence to show he committed the crime.

### Switching the Blame

This strategy is learned during childhood. Switching the blame to someone else might succeed in misleading the person who suspects you of wrongdoing. This is a relatively safe strategy to use, since it is not really important that the interrogator thinks the victim is to blame for their victimization. The suspect will not want to argue that point and insist that they are responsible. In fact, it is to the benefit of the suspect that the victim does "receive" responsibility for what occurred. In cases of sexual assault, the interrogator can switch the blame from the suspect onto the victim. Had the victim not dressed in such an inviting manner, the suspect would not have been encouraged to have sexual contact. With child molestation, suspects seem to have one common theme: their wives are at fault.

154

**Real-Life Scenario:**

*A young girl reported to her schoolteacher that her father sexually molested her. During the suspect's interview, he initially denied any such conduct. He also reported that his marriage was in jeopardy and that his wife was engaged in extramarital activities. The interrogator then switched the blame for the sexual molestation onto the wife, since her abandonment of her duties as a wife caused undue stress upon the suspect. The wife's behavior also place the daughter into the position of housewife, which also includes sexual contact. The suspect confessed to the crime, agreeing that his wife was negligent in her relationship as his wife.*

## Downplaying the Offense

Not all crimes are major events. This technique is useful when confronting a suspect about a relatively minor theft or another such offense. The interrogator needs to ask the suspect, "Is *this* what your life is worth?" Surely, someone's life is more important than the theft of money. The suspect fears incarceration and places the importance of the money below it. The rationale for this technique is that we all believe we have self-worth and we cannot place a monetary value on it. The answer to the question "Is *this* what your life is worth?" is no, it's not. The suspect's life is worth much more than he stole. For this reason, the interrogator can downplay the importance of the theft. The money is insignificant compared to his life, and there should be no fear in admitting that the theft occurred as suspected. By questioning the suspect's self-worth, a challenge has been offered. To prevent embarrassment, the suspect needs to agree that the money is not important and that he can discuss the theft. Some suspects may be insulted that the interrogator implies that money is more important than they are. In crimes of violence, where little or no injury occurred, the offense can be downplayed based on the suspect's actions. Obviously, it would be difficult to downplay the significance of a murder or rape. But in cases where little injury occurred, it can be seen as insignificant as compared to more serious assaults.

**Real-Life Scenario:**

*A rapist was terrorizing the Savannah, Georgia area during 1987. The modus operandi used by the rapist to subdue his intended victims was to fire a handgun into the air. During his interrogation, it was noted that he was an extremely large man. In order to downplay the crime, the author pointed out that with his size and strength, and using a handgun, he could have injured or killed the victims at whim. He was to be commended on his ability to control himself, since his actions were not as serious as they could have been. The suspect agreed and confessed that he had no intention of actually injuring the victims. The suspect claimed that he used the handgun for its shock value.*

## Logic

Most of the decisions made during our day are based upon logic. We weigh the pros and cons to decide the best course of action. It is often difficult to argue with logic since it is clear and convincing. Criminal investigations are, for the most part, conducted upon logical and rational thought. For example, a crime scene must "work" before a victim can be believed beyond a doubt. We examine the scene and evidence to decide whether the incident could have logically occurred as reported. This holds true in interrogations as well. Suspects who deny committing crimes will present an alibi for their actions during the time frame of the incident. Some suspects will present hastily formulated alibis, while others will have time to think of a reasonable sounding alibi. In the total absence of evidence indicating responsibility, most alibis are sufficient to refute suspicion. Many suspects present alibis that cannot be verified or refuted. When a suspect claims to have been "home alone," it is the interrogator's job to logically convince the suspect that the evidence is overwhelming and that being home alone is insufficient to deny guilt. The suspect has presented an unverifiable alibi; therefore it is placed aside by the interrogator in favor of physical or testimonial evidence that *can* be verified.

### Real-Life Scenario:
*During the commission of a burglary, a suspect cut himself climbing through a broken window. He also dropped his wallet as he left the scene. The alibi presented during his interrogation was that he often walked past the scene and must have dropped his wallet on the day in question. He offered no names of those who could verify this alibi. Rather than concentrate on the* lack *of evidence supporting his alibi, the interrogator applied logic concerning the wallet and blood. The interrogator presented his logical portrayal of the event. The suspect was present at the scene at* some *point, his wallet was found at the scene, his blood was found on the window glass (as this occurred prior to DNA technology, only ABO blood grouping was available), and he had no witnesses to support his claim. The suspect agreed that logically, it appeared that he had some involvement in*

*the incident. Without further interrogation, the suspect admitted that he committed the burglary.*

It will be noted that this interrogation technique is very similar to that of *overwhelming* evidence, which will be discussed next. The difference between the two techniques is that there is *insufficient evidence* in the logical approach as compared to overwhelming evidence. The logical approach simply "makes sense," whereas overwhelming evidence is virtually undeniable. The aim of this interrogation technique is to have the suspect agree with the interrogator that he was responsible for the crime.

**Overwhelming Evidence**

As with the logical technique, applying overwhelming evidence during an interrogation will give the suspect the belief that it is futile to deny committing a crime. This technique is useful when sufficient evidence is collected indicating someone's complicity. In the logical technique, a lack of evidence existed to convince the suspect that his involvement in the crime has been proven. However, in the face of overwhelming evidence, the only issue is that of futility. The interrogator simply enumerates the items of evidence to the suspect. How can the suspect deny involvement against such odds? While offering the abundant evidence, the interrogator then shows finality to the interrogation. Closing the case file shows finality, as it is no longer needed for the interrogation. A click of the pen and placing it away also shows up the suspect that all is in order and no further discussion is needed except to "wrap up" the loose ends. Once the mountain of evidence is offered and finality is demonstrated, the interrogator then suggests the meeting can be completed by documenting what is known (his complicity). This technique, as with many others, requires a degree of acting by the interrogator. The suspect may continue to deny involvement. The interrogator will meet these denials with the steadfast belief that the evidence overwhelmingly proves complicity and that further denials are pointless. To further support the belief that there is overwhelming evidence against the suspect, props, which will be discussed later in this chapter, can be used to convince the suspect that there is no question regarding responsibility.

## Sympathy

Not all offenders commit crimes without a degree of sorrow. Crimes between relations are often emotional. Child and spouse abuse are emotional crimes, and the offenders often feel badly about their actions. When a suspect displays sorrow, the interrogator provides sympathy. Care must be taken when suspects begin to cry. Some interrogators believe that comforting a crying suspect will gain their cooperation in obtaining a confession. However, suspects often use crying as a tactic to delay the questioning. In uncomfortable situations, we use various actions to delay the inevitable. Coughing, straightening an item of clothing, checking the time on our watch, and crying will temporarily provide us with a short reprieve, and give us a chance to think of a solution to our problem. Supplying a crying suspect with tissues will assist him in slowing down the questioning, or stopping it temporarily. A tissue can make an excellent defense barrier when used to cover the face. To prevent this tactic, the crying suspect should be left to cry *without* the aid of tissues or time to "compose" him or herself. Questioning should continue as if the suspect were not crying. This can be done with sympathy, and if the suspect's sorrow is legitimate, then it may work to the interrogator's advantage. If the sorrow and crying is deceptive, the interrogator has not lost precious time by allowing the suspect to stall the questioning. Suspects who display genuine sorrow will accept the interrogator's offer of sympathy with sincere statements. They may indicate that they are sorry for the offense, or for the injury upon the victim. False sorrow will be shallow, without any admission of involvement. The suspect providing false sorrow will feel sorry for themselves and not the victim. They attempt to switch attention away from the victimized and onto themselves as the wrongfully accused.

## Bragging

Many detectives feel that suspects often need to tell someone about their crimes. In instances where murders occur, it is a fair bet that the suspect has confided in someone. This could be for several reasons: guilt, sorrow, or perhaps, bragging. In gang-related killings, the act of murder is viewed as a "rite of passage" into the gang. It is an act to be proud of, and everyone needs to learn of it. These types of offenders are immature and need to brag about their deeds to gain the "respect" of others. Along with this "respect" comes the fear of the offender by others.

During interrogations, certain offenders would love to brag of their crimes. If the interrogator is successful in convincing the offender that they are impressive in their acts, the suspect may begin to brag about their accomplishments.

**Real-Life Scenario:**
*When the author interviewed the serial rapist in Savannah, Georgia, this particular technique produced a confession. The following is an excerpt from the exchange:*
*Interrogator: Eric, you need to keep one thing in mind, you're a big guy, and very strong. You had the power to either injure or kill those women you kidnapped, but you didn't. That took great restraint. You were in control of the situation. You should consider yourself really lucky to be in that much control of yourself. You could have killed them if you wanted to, right?*
*Suspect: That's right, I could have killed them, but I decided to let them live and just scare them.*

In cases of sexual assault, the offender is interested in the power he has over the victim, not the act of sex. By providing the suspect with the proper bolstering, the interrogator can be successful in gaining an admission of guilt. Crimes against persons often consist of a power struggle, the strong over the weak.

In other crimes, such as larceny, fraud, or non-violent serial offenses, the issue is often that of skill and ability rather than physical power. Habitual criminals take pride in their ability to commit crimes without discovery. These offenders often develop unusual techniques that only they are aware of. For these reasons, getting a suspect to brag about their unique abilities can often lead to an admission or confession.

**Real-Life Scenario:**
*Interrogator: How did you figure out the schedule of that courier? That's pretty impressive. I'm sure we can learn a lot from you.*
*Suspect: It was simple; all you have to do is show up early and wait. They always change their schedule, but eventually they return to the same hours of delivery.*

## Guilt

We all have guilt. This is not the legal guilt found by the courts, but the personal emotional guilt felt from wrongful actions. The question in this technique is *where* does the guilt lie? Many offenders can commit crimes without feeling guilt at all, or they are successful in rationalizing away their guilt by placing the blame upon the victim. The more time that passes between the crime and the interrogation, the more successful the suspect will be in reducing his feelings of guilt.

## Real-Life Scenario:
*A military suspect wrongfully appropriated a government truck from an installation and drove it to his hometown. The preliminary investigation quickly identified the soldier as a likely suspect. Immediately upon his return to the installation, the suspect was interrogated about the truck. Guilt bothered the suspect so much, that he could not sit down, and continually paced back and forth. With minimal questioning, the suspect confessed to taking the truck for his personal use.*

In some instances, there are multiple suspects. Long delays between the crime and interrogation will afford the suspects a chance to fortify each other, which will prevent guilt from taking over. If this occurs, the interrogator will have additional work to isolate the suspect's guilt and apply it effectively.

The interrogator's goal is to identify *what* the suspect feels guilty about. The interrogator's impression of what the suspect should feel guilty about may not be accurate at all. The essence of the guilt is found by applying blame to the suspect for the various outcomes of the crime. This may be a long, slow process; however, once the appropriate guilt issue is identified, the interrogation can then be focused. What guilt issues are commonly found? The issues are many: the victim's pain and suffering, responsibility for future events, moralistic issues, such as violating religious tenets against crime, and others. Once the suspect's guilt is identified, it is important to establish just how the suspect feels. As the interrogator repeatedly reinforces the feelings of guilt, the suspect begins to regret his actions and desires to discuss how badly he feels. The goal of this technique is to convince the suspect that the guilt will lessen as details of what occurred are discussed. As the confession is developed, the interrogator again reinforces guilt upon the suspect, but asks if the suspect feels better as the information is discussed.

## Real-Life Scenario:

*A woman was interviewed as a suspect of aiding in a sexual assault. Even though the woman took a passive role in the assault, her testimony was needed to prosecute the primary assailant. It was suspected that the woman witnessed the assault and was withholding information to protect the assailant. During a three-hour interrogation the woman denied any knowledge of the incident, stating that the victim was lying. The woman then became quiet and only listened intently as the interrogator began to blame her for future assaults that would occur if the assailant were not prosecuted. This, being the essence of her guilt, resulted in her providing the interrogator with an extensive written statement implicating the assailant. An arrest and conviction resulted from her testimony.*

This suspect had little or no reaction to many of the interrogation techniques used by the interrogator, but her guilt induced a stressful reaction to the thought of future crimes.

## Silence

Silence is nothing, and there is much to say about nothing. Silence can work to the interrogator's advantage in a couple of ways. First, silence on the part of suspects may indicate their choosing to truthfully answer questions. By remaining silent, the suspect is actively accepting the interrogator as questioner. A suspect who plans on denying responsibility will want to verbally refute the suspicions. A common tactic in arguments is to continually talk without allowing the other party to respond. Other tactics are arguing and controlling the interrogation. As long as the suspect can prevent the interrogator from focusing on his responsibility for the crime, the suspect will be successful in avoiding a confession. Suspects who choose to remain silent will indicate this during the rights advisal. There is a marked difference between choosing to remain silent and becoming silent. During the early stages of the interrogation the suspect will deny complicity. Alibis are offered or others are blamed for the crime. As evidence mounts against the suspect the fear of being overwhelmed takes over. Guilty suspects will then want to learn as much as they can about the evidence against them. Innocent suspects, no matter what is said, will steadfastly deny all charges. Oftentimes the innocent suspect will interrupt the interrogator since continued questioning will fail to produce an admission of guilt. Being silent is the best way for the suspect to learn what evidence exists. As the suspect becomes silent, the interrogator knows that the suspect is weighing the advantages and disadvantages of confessing. How long does this silence last? This depends on whether or not the interrogator can find the issue to make the suspect want to confess. The suspect is simply waiting for the right rationale to be presented so a confession can be made.

Suspects often perceive silence on the part of the interrogator as active interrogation. During everyday conversations, the participants take turns providing or responding to statements. Cues are taken by verbal statements or by visible clues given by those involved. A simple nod or hand gesture will likely produce a verbal response from someone being addressed. By "giving someone the floor" we are accepting his or her temporary role as speaker. Listeners then respond as needed. It is important to use the silence technique at the right moment. In fact, the interrogator can test the suspect's susceptibility to respond to silence at any given point in the interrogation. This is done by asking a question and looking to the suspect expectantly. The verbal cue (question) and visual clue (expectant look) will tell the suspect that he is now the speaker, and information is required of him.

Silence must always follow an issue question or statement. If the interrogator were to sit there and just remain silent, the suspect would not receive any clues as to what is expected. Even though the suspect is not being guided by an issue question or statement, the suspect will still respond to the silent interrogator with some sort of comment. The issue question or statement will channel the suspect towards certain answers and information. Talkative suspects usually do not require prompting with silence. It is the quiet suspects that do. Once it is recognized that the suspect has become quiet, and has shown signs that he is considering what the interrogator is saying, the interrogator should choose to break the suspect's silence with an issues question.

**Real-Life Scenario:**
*Interrogator: The witnesses place you at the scene of the robbery. They say that you deliberately shot and wounded that store clerk.*
*Suspect: (silence)*

162

*Interrogator: You know, not all injuries are intentional. Sometimes people are injured by accident. You didn't mean to injure the store clerk, did you?*

Once the issue question is presented to the suspect, and immediately followed by silence, it is the interrogator's job to *remain silent*. This is often difficult since we are anxious for the question to be answered. In this scenario, the interrogator told the suspect that he was identified as the assailant and that he is being accused of *deliberately* shooting and wounding someone. He then offered the suspect an "out" by stating that not all injuries are intentional and that this could have been accidental. The silence that follows the crucial issue question "You didn't mean to injure the store clerk, did you?" must be maintained by the interrogator at all costs. A continuous gaze is maintained, even if the suspect breaks off eye contact. Patience will eventually solicit *some* response from the suspect. Many suspects will break their silence after a short pause to see if the interrogator will continue to speak, which may help them delay answering questions.

There are three possible responses to the interrogator's silence. First, the suspect may continue to be silent. Some suspects see the silence as a challenge and will choose to meet it. The interrogator returns the silence in an expectant manner. If the suspect continues his silence, a visual clue may be needed. The interrogator can raise his hands and look at the suspect in a questioning manner. Verbal cues should be used only after the suspect fails to respond to the visual clues.

*Interrogator: The witnesses place you at the scene of the robbery. They say that you deliberately shot and wounded that store clerk.*
*Suspect: (silence)*
*Interrogator: You know, not all injuries are intentional. Sometimes people are injured by accident. You didn't mean to injure the store clerk, did you?*
*Suspect: (silence)*
*Interrogator: (leans forward, places pen on the desk and gestures by raising his hands with continued eye contact)*
*Suspect: (silence)*
*Interrogator: (following a prolonged silence) It* was *intentional?*

In this version, the suspect failed to respond to the issue question. The interrogator waited but did not receive any reply. Visual clues were offered. Leaning forward and placing the pen on the desk are symbolic that nothing else is going to happen until the question is answered. The hand gestures reinforced these actions. The suspect was either considering answering the question or refusing to do so. To break the silence, the visual cues were followed by a verbal cue intended to push the suspect into talking. Not only was the verbal cue used to make the suspect respond, it also contained the most unfavorable option, that the suspect intentionally injured someone. The interrogator also stressed the word *intentional* to convince the suspect that his silence indicates this to be true. Most, if not all, suspects will make a response in this situation.

Second, the suspect may attempt to end the uncomfortable silence with delaying tactics. Here the interrogator must recognize what is happening and maintain the correct focus.

*Interrogator: The witnesses place you at the scene of the robbery. They say that you deliberately shot and wounded that store clerk.*
*Suspect: (silence)*
*Interrogator: You know, not all injuries are intentional. Sometimes people are injured by accident. You didn't mean to injure the store clerk, did you?*
*Interrogator: (silence)*
*Suspect: Intentional? Is that what they said?*
*Interrogator: (silence)*

The suspect ended the period of silence, but did so with a question. If the interrogator answers this question, the interrogation is delayed, providing the suspect with time to think of a good response. This situation is best confronted with continued silence; remember, the *interrogator* asks the questions, and the *suspect* answers them.

The third possible response is a period of denial or admission. However, by applying silence the interrogator was successful in getting the suspect to talk. If the suspect continues to deny, other interrogation techniques are used. If the suspect makes an admission, then it is developed further.

**Props**

Props are used to lend credibility to the interrogator's statements. There is good news about using props, and there is bad news. The good news is that the suspect has no control over what the prop is, or its origin. A prop can be used to convince the suspect that there is sufficient evidence to prove his guilt, and that further denials are needless. The bad news is that the interrogator was not present during the crime and really does not possess all of the details. Further, the interrogator does not know what the suspect knows. The obvious danger, then, is that the suspect will realize that the prop is false and the interrogator is lying. Once this occurs, restoring credibility may be very difficult. There are various types of props that can be used by the interrogator. The rule to using these props is *never use a prop that can be refuted by the suspect*.

Fingerprints are found at most crime scenes, although many of these are partial or fragmented prints. Everyone knows that a fingerprint can establish identification. Using a fingerprint already prepared before the interrogation, the interrogator can produce it to suggest that the suspect's identity can be easily established. The fingerprint prop is often a dangerous gambit unless the interrogator knows that the suspect did not use gloves during the crime.

Case documents within the case file, which should be visible throughout the interrogation, can be used as a prop without much concern for discovery. The suspect expects that all information collected during the investigation will be kept in the file. It is also logical to refuse to allow the suspect to review the contents of the file. So the value of this technique is "What is in that file?" As the suspect answers questions and denies complicity, the interrogator can "refer" to the file for the "correct" information.

**Real-Life Scenario:**
*Interrogator: What time did you arrive home on the night of the murder?*
*Suspect: I'm sure I returned home between eight and nine.*
*Interrogator: Are you sure?*
*Suspect: Absolutely, I wasn't near the victim's house.*
*Interrogator: Well, that's not what the witnesses said (picks up the case file and reads, glancing occasionally at the suspect). What time did you get home again?*

Whether or not there are witnesses is immaterial. The suspect can only take the interrogator at his word. To lend more credibility to this technique, the interrogator can close the file with a flourish, place it on the desk and tell the suspect that the evidence is clear. The suspect has only to wonder what evidence exists in that file. During breaks in the interrogation, all case documents should be removed to preclude the suspect from reading their contents.

Who can be more convincing that someone you trust? In situations where there are multiple suspects, one can become a prop for another. Multiple suspects are always interviewed separately and preferably at the same time. While both suspects deny the crime, one interrogator can bring his suspect to the other interrogation room to "verify" the suspect's identify. The "verifying" suspect is told that he needs to verify the identify of the suspect in the other room. The suspect is brought to the interrogation room, and once inside is asked, "Is that Jim?" Obviously, since the suspects know one another, his response will be, "Yes, that's him." The suspect being viewed only sees his trusted accomplice "fingering" him for the crime, and probably making a deal with the authorities. To enhance this technique, the interrogator of the viewed suspect continues to reinforce that the suspect's identification as being responsible for the crime has been established. In order to defend himself, the suspect now has the option to blame the other suspect, thus revealing his own complicity. This technique is fairly flexible. People whom the suspect does not know can also enter the room to "verify" his identity.

**Real-Life Scenario:**
*Interrogator: We know you were there.*
*Suspect: I was not there. I had nothing to do with this.*
*Second Interrogator: (enters room with a "witness"). Is this the person you saw?*
*Witness: Yes, that's the man I saw. (Leaves with second interrogator).*
*Interrogator: As I was saying, we know you were there. That witness saw you and has now identified you as being there. Did you go there with the intent of stealing that property?*

Almost anything can be used as a prop in an interrogation. The only caution is to be sure that the prop is believable and irrefutable. There is almost nothing worse than presenting a prop to a suspect who immediately refutes its relevance.

In some instances, it is possible to use imaginary people as props, meaning that there is no prop at all. This type of prop can be used if the interrogator feels certain that the suspect will not challenge the bluff, which is exactly what this prop is. If the suspect does challenge it, then the interrogator's credibility and case will be damaged. Most suspects will not want to be identified as criminals, and even find it embarrassing to appear before others in that capacity. The more the suspect has to lose, the more likely this prop will produce positive results.

**Real-Life Scenario:**
*The author received a complaint that a store clerk was selling alcohol to minors. Since there was no demonstrative evidence of this, an impromptu interview was conducted.*
*Interrogator: We received a report that you have been selling alcohol to minors here in your store. Is that true?*
*Suspect: Me? Sell alcohol to minors? No way. That's illegal; I wouldn't do that.*
*Interrogator: Several juveniles have reported purchasing alcohol from you.*
*Suspect: They're lying! Who are you going to believe?*
*Interrogator: OK. I think we can resolve this issue rather quickly. I have four parents out there in your store right now who are willing to point out the person responsible for selling the alcohol to children. They actually witnessed these sales. Let's go talk to them, OK?*
*Suspect: Who are they?*
*Interrogator: Angry parents.*
*Suspects: OK, look, I did it. But I was just being nice to the kids, that's all. I never meant any harm.*

Several things occurred during this exchange. First, the suspect denied the charge and offered an explanation as to why she wouldn't sell alcohol to minors. Second, upon further evidence, the suspect again denied the charge, adding that minors were not to be believed. In either case, the interrogator failed to engage in discussion about her rationalizations, and immediately presented a prop, or the fictitious witnesses. The logic is that a truly innocent clerk would be glad to speak to the angry parents. However, the guilty clerk would obviously shun this opportunity.

**Necessity**

Some crimes are committed out of pure necessity. This does not relieve the suspect of responsibility, since one person's necessity is not society's problem. Rather than condemn a person who steals for his personal needs, the interrogator should support the necessity of the crime. What issues make a crime "necessary"? Fear, hunger, anxiety, intoxication, poverty, peer pressure, and other situations tend to make a suspect feel that committing the crime was necessary, and therefore it should be understood and excused by the authorities. Whether the crime is excusable or not is a question for the courts to decide. Gang-related crimes are often the product of peer pressure. How many times have investigators heard the tale of woe that if not for the crime, the suspect would be beaten or killed for failing to comply with gang rules? Suspects commit crimes by convincing themselves that they are "OK," and therefore necessary. Once the interrogator supports this belief, suspects are more apt to explain their behavior with a confession.

**Real-Life Scenario:**
*Interrogator: It's believed that you shot and killed the victim because you hated him. Is that what happened, or did you have to kill him in order to defend yourself?*
*Suspect: I was scared to death. I thought he was going to kill me, so the only thing I could do was to get him first.*
*Interrogator: So you had to defend yourself. I can understand that. You're allowed to defend yourself.*

**Indifference**

Suspects who have inflated egos relish receiving admiration or awe from those they attempt to impress with their crimes. These suspects will brag to their acquaintances about their skill and bravery. To them, the crime is worthwhile as long as they can receive some sort of gratification from telling others about what occurred. This technique can be used to make this type of suspect want to discuss their crime. Obviously, they will not want to discuss the crime with the interrogator, just other criminals. They would love to brag to the interrogator but for the possibility of incarceration. To use this technique, the interrogator feigns disinterest in the suspect's abilities. The crime that was committed was not a "big deal" and not at all impressive. This technique also uses the technique of downplaying the offense, but in a different manner. The downplaying technique convinces the suspect that the offense was not that egregious, and that he should confess. This technique offers an insult to the suspect, challenging his abilities. Suspects who accept this dare will want to set the record straight and talk about their crimes.

## Religion

Many suspects are religious. In fact, many offenders are members of the clergy. The obvious caveat to this technique is that interrogators should never give the impression that they are clergy. As stated earlier, this would be unethical conduct, since clergy/penitent discussions are privileged. What should the interrogator do if the suspect wants to interject religion into the interrogation? Would it be wise to prevent this type of discussion? Many interrogators may feel uncomfortable discussing religion. Some interrogators who are religious may find it easy to discuss. In either event, the interrogator should accept the religious rhetoric offered by the suspect. Keep in mind that, while offering religious statements, the suspect is talking to the interrogator, which is a positive sign. Many religious discussions become debates concerning personal philosophies, which should be avoided at all costs, as it detracts from the purpose of the interrogation. Instead, the interrogator should focus on the suspect's statements while applying assertions that the suspect's beliefs are important to the outcome of the investigation, and that confessing would be the right thing to do. In some instances, religious suspects may want to pray for forgiveness along with the interrogator. Even though the interrogator feels uncomfortable or is not religious, cooperating with the suspect may bring about a confession. Caution should be exercised, since the suspect may want to control the interrogation using religion.

## Repetitive statements

The technique of repetitive statements, which is used to test the information supplied by a suspect, can be used to show the suspect that efforts to lie about a crime are futile. The suspect is asked to present his alibi in as much detail as possible. No interrogation takes place at this point, since the object of this technique is to allow the suspect to weave a tale of innocence. After the initial rendition is completed, the suspect is asked to repeat portions of the information, but this time in a different order. In many cases, the suspect will fabricate the alibi during the discussion. If that occurs, it is unlikely the suspect will recall all the details of his alibi. As the alibi begins to unravel and the sequence of events changes, the interrogator then impresses upon the suspect that lying is futile and that a confession is the best route to take. Other techniques can then be applied to the suspect once it is demonstrated that deception was obvious.

## "Third-degree" tactics

The classic third-degree tactic, or what is commonly referred to as the "Mutt and Jeff" technique, is considered to be unethical and unprofessional. In this technique one of the interrogators plays the "nice guy," while his partner plays the role of the "mean guy." The interrogation begins with the nice interrogator attempting to get information from the suspect without any force. He is nice to the suspect. The nice interrogator also acts quite laid back and understanding of the suspect's situation. Most suspects will see this interrogator as an easy pushover, and will continue to deny involvement in any crime. The suspect will believe he can control the interrogation with this ineffectual interrogator. At some point in the interrogation, the mean interrogator enters to listen to the suspect's denials. This interrogator then displays a short temper while accusing the suspect of being a liar. The accusation continues for a short period of time, usually ending with a promise to put the suspect in prison. At the height of the accusations, the mean interrogator leaves the room, never to return. Obviously, the suspect is flustered, and perhaps angry with the mean interrogator. The nice interrogator then attempts to calm the suspect by agreeing that the mean interrogator was off base with his remarks, and that the suspect does not have to speak to him. In fact, the suspect should talk only to the nice interrogator, who is now "on his side." The suspect is told that the other interrogator would easily put the suspect into prison, regardless of what happened and why it happened. However, the nice interrogator offers to consider what happened since he is more rational in his understanding. The unprofessional aspect of this technique is that it contains threats of punishment if the suspect does not correctly answer questions. If a suspect were to confess in light of these threats, the confession could clearly be deemed inadmissible. Other "Mutt and Jeff" techniques offer different unprofessional actions, such as yelling, cursing, demeaning the suspect, and unlawfully applying physical discomfort. Mistreatment of suspects is never acceptable.

## Tandem interviewers

While on the topic of multiple interrogators, mention should be made of tandem interrogators. Interrogations should involve only one interrogator at a time. There are some excellent reasons for this. First, using multiple interrogators suggests the possibility of coercion. In some instances, interrogations have been conducted with more than two interrogators, all firing questions at the suspect. It is easy to see how a suspect will regard this as coercion.

During a final examination of the author's interrogation students, it was noted that the students opted to use two interrogators rather than one. This was interesting, since at no time were double interrogators used during the interrogations class. This tactic was apparently used more for the comfort of the students rather than obtaining a confession from their suspect. The interrogations were difficult, since the two student interrogators were not properly coordinated in their effort. The suspects were successful in confusing the issue under investigation by addressing both student interrogators about different issues. Only when a single student interrogator replaced the team did the interrogation return to its proper format.

The second reason using two interrogators is a bad idea is that the suspect may perceive the team as being unorganized. Prior planning is required in the event two interrogators are used. One interrogator must be the lead questioner. Disagreements or conflicts between the interrogators will defeat the effects the interrogation may have on the suspect. The proper concept for tandem interrogators is to have one conduct the questioning and the other record information. In this regard, the suspect is aware that the questioner is the primary interrogator, and that there are no conflicts between the interrogators.

The optimum situation is to have interrogators replace one another in the event the interrogation stops producing results. It is common for interrogators to lose their connection with the suspect, or have a personality conflict occur. Other interrogators can step in to complete the interrogation without giving the suspect the notion that the effort was flawed.

**Recommended punishment**

Since we know that all suspects would like to prevent their own incarceration, it stands to reason that if they were given the chance to recommend their own punishment, it would be minimal. Innocent suspects would likely recommend that the actual offender be punished to the limit of the law. This technique can be used at any point in the interrogation. The suspect is simply asked, "What sort of punishment should the person who did this receive?" If the suspect recommends an unreasonably lenient punishment, then this would be indicative of a guilty suspect. Note that not all guilty suspects will choose the leniency over the punishment.  Some suspects will recommend severe punishment, expecting that leniency would indicate their unreasonableness.

### Mirroring

The next time you are in a social situation speaking to someone, watch for the theory of mirroring.  Mirroring occurs when we are speaking to someone we identify with.  When we mirror, we copy the other person's behavior.  One person may cross his arms, or place his hands in his pockets; the other may follow suit.  It would not be unusual to see a group of men engaged in a discussion while mirroring each other's stance.  Mirroring is the congruence between speakers.  Understanding this, we can use mirroring upon the suspect, thus helping the suspect "identify" with the interrogator.  If the suspect leans over with his arms on his knees, looking down in a rejected manner, then the interrogator should mirror him in the same fashion.  This tell the suspect that "I'm with you in this," and provides the suspect with a connection to the interrogator.

### Choices

At some point in the interrogation, the interrogator may elect to give the suspect some choices.  However, these choices are quite limited.  The rationale of a choice question is to give the suspect the liberty of choosing a certain outcome based upon the information presented by the interrogator.  This technique can be equated to choosing the "lesser of two evils."  Regardless of the choice made by the suspect, the result is the same, an admission of guilt.  The interrogator can also control the suspect's choice.  The interrogator will most likely believe that the suspect was responsible for certain behaviors based upon the evidence of the case.  The suspect, of course, will deny this behavior.  To bring about an admission, the interrogator provides the suspect with a set of choices, those being the suspected behavior and a more serious set of circumstances.

### Real-Life Scenario:
*Two men were involved in an argument, during which one produced a knife.  The unarmed man attempted to flee during the scuffle, which resulted in him being seriously injured.  During the suspect's interrogation, the interrogator offered a set of choices.  The choices were stabbing the victim out of anger or attempting to murder the victim.  The suspect claimed that*

*the stabbing was accidental, even though the victim's description of the incident refuted that claim. When offered the choices, the suspect vehemently denied attempting to murder the victim, admitting that he attacked the victim out of his uncontrolled anger. He admitted that he only intended minor injury, rather than the serious injury that resulted from the fight.*

This technique can also be used in other types of crimes. In cases of larceny, the amount of stolen money or property can become part of the choices.

*Interrogator: Our investigation has indicated your involvement in the theft of $1000 from the company. The evidence is pretty clear and convincing.*
*Suspect: I didn't steal that money.*
*Interrogator: That's not what the evidence proves. In fact ,over the last few months about $5,000 has been stolen from the company. Did you take that as well? Or was it just the $1,000? I'm sure we can arrange repayment to correct this situation.*
*Suspect: I only took the $1,000. I have no idea what happened to the rest of the money.*

### Concluding the Interrogation

There are two possible outcomes to every interrogation. The suspect either confesses to the crime or does not. In either situation, it is always advisable to conclude the interrogation in such a way as to leave the door open for more questioning in the future. If the suspect denies any responsibility, the interrogator then affirms that the investigation will continue and that evidence will be collected to further establish his or her guilt. Offenders who maintain their innocence will most likely agree to be reinterviewed for two reasons: first, to continue their appearance of innocence, and second, to learn what new evidence is found to indicate their guilt. Those who have confessed to the crime and rendered a written or oral statement may not have provided all details of the crime. In many cases, reinterviews are needed to explain new evidence or to develop investigative leads when there are multiple suspects involved. Regardless of the situation upon concluding the interrogation, it is always to the benefit of the interrogator to end the meeting in a professional and courteous manner.

## Chapter Summary

The following are the most common interrogation techniques: how investigations work, mistake, lying, switching the blame, downplaying the offense, logic, overwhelming evidence, sympathy, bragging, guilt, silence, props, necessity, repetitive statements, religion, third-degree tactics (not recommended), indifference, mirroring behavior, tandem interrogators, recommended punishment, and choice questions. Interrogators do not use these techniques individually, but in a combination. Once a suspect adequately responds to a technique, the interrogator can continue using it to obtain the confession. Once the interrogation is concluded, regardless of the outcome, the interrogator should treat the suspect in a courteous manner. It is not unusual to reinterview suspects at a later date. The proper closure will assist in gaining a subsequent interview in the future.

# CHAPTER ELEVEN

# TESTIFYING IN COURT

*Reprinted with permission from*
**Criminal Investigation**, Eighth Edition
*by* Wayne W. Bennett and Kären M. Hess
© 2007 Wadsworth/Thomson Learning

## Testifying under Direct Examination

Rutledge (*Courtroom*, p. 15) asserts: "No matter how brilliant the investigation, how careful the arrest, and how thorough the report, if an officer isn't just as competent on the stand as he is in the field, he is just processing bodies." He (p. 12) stresses: "You are on trial, too—your credibility, your professionalism, your knowledge, your competence, your judgment, your conduct in the field, your use of force, your adherence to official policies, your observance of the defendant's rights—they're all on trial."

As you enter the courtroom, keep in mind your goal. It is probably in line with the thinking of Van Brocklin (p. 48): "The goal for officers in their courtroom confrontations is the same as in their street confrontations—win." But surprisingly, Van Brocklin (p. 44) does not mean win the case:

> The "win" for every honest officer in every courtroom
> confrontation is as simple as it is difficult: at the end of their
> testimony, when the last question has been answered, the jury
> must find them *credible*. Credibility is the degree to which the
> jury believes a witness. That's it. That's the only goal, the only
> win, the only job for the testifying officer—to be believed by
> the jury.

First impressions are critical. Know what you are doing when you enter the courtroom. When your name is called, answer "Here" or "Present" and move directly to the front of the courtroom. Do not walk between the prosecutor and the judge; go behind the attorneys. Garland and Stuckey (p.

509) caution that officers should never walk in front of the judge or between the judge and the attorney's tables. This area, called **the well**, is off-limits and is to be entered only if the judge so directs or permission is granted. Traditionally, the area is a sword's length and was intended for the judge's protection.

Walk confidently; the jurors are there to hear the facts from you. If your investigation has been thorough and properly conducted, the jury will give a great deal of weight to your testimony.

If you have notes or a report, carry them in a clean manila file folder in your left hand so your right hand is free for taking the oath. Taking the oath in court is basically the same as taking your oath to office. Stand straight and face the clerk of the court, holding the palm of your hand toward the clerk. Use a clear, firm voice to answer "I do" to the question "Do you promise to tell the truth, the whole truth, and nothing but the truth, so help you God?" Do not look at the judge, either legal counsel, or the jury.

Sit with your back straight but in a comfortable position, usually with your hands folded in your lap or held on the arms of the chair. Do not move the chair around or fidget, because this is distracting. Hold notes and other reports in your lap. If the reports are bulky, many experts on testifying recommend placing them under the chair until needed.

The witness chair in all courtrooms is positioned so you can face the judge, legal counsel, jury, or the audience, depending on to whom your answers are directed. In most instances, if the judge asks you a question, look directly at the judge to answer. If either the prosecutor or defense counsel asks you a question, look directly at the jury to give your answer. The prosecutor will ask you to state your name, department, and position. As you respond, keep in mind the types of statements that are not admissible.

Testify only to what you actually saw, heard, or did, not what you believe, heard from others, or were told about. You can testify to what a defendant told you directly, but any other statements must be testified to by the person making them.

Preparation is the key to being a good witness. After a review of your personal notes and all relevant reports, you will be familiar with the case and can "tell it like it is." This will come across well to the jury and establish your credibility.

How you speak is often as important as what you say. Talk slowly, deliberately, and loudly enough to be heard by everyone. Never use obscenity or vulgarity unless the court requests a suspect's or victim's exact words. In such cases, inform the court before you answer that the answer requested includes obscenity or vulgarity.

Ignore the courtroom's atmosphere. Devote your entire attention to giving truthful answers to questions. Answer all questions directly and politely with "yes" or "no" unless asked to relate an action taken, an observation made, or information told to you directly by the defendant. Refer to the judge as "your honor" and to the defendant as "the defendant." Do not volunteer information. Instead, let the prosecution decide whether to pursue a particular line of questioning.

Take a few seconds after hearing the question to form your answer. If the counsel or the court objects to a question, wait until instructed to proceed. If it takes some time for the judge to rule on an objection, ask to have the question repeated.

Reviewing the case thoroughly before your courtroom appearance does not mean that you should memorize specific dates, addresses, or spellings of names and places. Memorization can lead to confusion. Instead use notes to help avoid contradictions and inconsistencies. An extemporaneous answer is better received by the judge and jury than one that sounds rehearsed.

Using notes too much detracts from your testimony, weakens your presentation, and gives the impression you have not adequately prepared for the case. It can also lead to having your notes introduced into the record. If, as you refer to your notes, you discover you have given erroneous testimony such as an incorrect date or time, notify the court immediately. Do not try to cover up the discrepancy. Everyone makes mistakes. If you admit them in a professional manner, little harm results. Do not hesitate to admit that you do not know the answer to a question or that you do not understand a question. Never bluff or attempt to fake your way through an answer.

In addition, be aware of certain phrases that may leave a negative impression on the jury. Phrases such as "I believe" or "to the best of my recollection" will not impress a jury. Do not argue or use sarcasm, witticisms, or "smart" answers. Be direct, firm, and positive. Be courteous, whether in response to a question from the prosecutor or an objection from the defense or the judge. Do not hesitate to give information favorable to the defendant. Your primary responsibility is to state what you know about the case.

If asked to identify evidence with your personal mark, take time to examine the item thoroughly. Make sure that all marks are accounted for and that your mark has not been altered. A rapid identification may make a bad impression on the jury and may lead you into an erroneous identification.

**Nonverbal Factors**

Do not underestimate the power of nonverbal factors as you testify. Over 25 years ago, Dr. Albert Mehrabian conducted his famous, often-cited study at UCLA and concluded that communication is made up of several components consisting of:

- *What* is said—the actual words spoken (7 percent of the total message communicated)
- *How* it is said—tone of voice, pitch, modulation, and the like (38 percent of the message)
- *Nonverbal factors*—body language, gestures, demeanor (55 percent)

Thus, the bulk of a message is conveyed not through which words are used but in how they are delivered. Never overlook the importance of how you present information and nonverbal factors when testifying. Important nonverbal elements include dress, eye contact, posture, gestures, mannerisms, and facial expressions.

Avoid actions associated with deception such as putting a hand over your mouth, rubbing your nose, preening, straightening your hair, buttoning your coat, picking lint off your clothing, or tugging at your shirt or a pant leg.

## Testifying under Cross-Examination

It is understandable that an investigator would consider the defense attorney's cross-examination as an attack on the prosecution's case. However, according to Van Brocklin (p. 46), investigators' *attitudes* determine their testimony style and their body language. During cross-examination, while the defense attorney attempts to impeach your testimony or at least undermine your credibility, Van Brocklin (p. 48) enumerates behaviors that juror comments from posttrial interviews indicate weaken a witness's credibility:

- Uses a defensive or evasive tone of voice
- Appears ill at ease or nervous
- Avoids eye contact
- Crosses arms defensively across chest
- Quibbles over common terms
- Sits stiffly
- Looks to attorney for assistance during cross-examination
- Cracks jokes inappropriately
- Uses lots of "ah's" or "uh's"

In contrast, jurors have noted that the following behaviors enhance credibility:

- Displays an even temperament on direct and cross
- Doesn't become angry or defensive when pressed
- Appears relaxed and at ease
- Is likeable and polite
- Maintains eye contact with attorney and jury
- Is not affected by interruptions or objection

Rutledge (*Courtroom*, p. 60) notes: "You're not an advocate—you're a witness. Don't try to thwart the defense lawyer." Cross-examination is usually the most difficult part of testifying. "The defense lawyer's most important task is to destroy your credibility—to make you look like you're either a ...bungler, a liar, or both. How does he do that? He attacks you. He tricks you. He outsmarts you. He confuses you. He frustrates you. He annoys you. He probes for your most vulnerable characteristics" (Rutledge, p. 118). How does this make officers feel?

Van Brocklin (pp. 46-47) suggests that when officers are given a word-association test and the words *defense attorney* are given, "Exclamations fly—*snake, shark, weasel, slime, dishonest, deceptive, liar*, and several that need not be printed." According to Van Brocklin this negative attitude explains why an officer can do a competent job in the investigation, be truthful, and still not be believed by the jury. If jurors perceive that an investigator is acting defensively, they may think that the investigator is not testifying truthfully: "Jurors think that only a guilty person—a person with something to hide—acts defensively." The key is to recognize this tendency and remain professional and objective.

The defense attorney will attempt to cast doubt on your direct testimony in an effort to win an acquittal for the defendant. Know the methods of attack for cross-examination to avoid being trapped.

During cross-examination the defense attorney may:
- Be disarmingly friendly or intimidatingly rude.
- Attack your credibility and impartiality.
- Attack your investigative skill.
- Attempt to force contradictions or inconsistencies.
- Ask leading questions or deliberately misquote you.
- Ask for a simple answer to a complex question.
- Use rapid-fire questioning.
- Use the silent treatment.

The defense attorney can be extremely friendly, hoping to put you off guard by making the questioning appear to be just a friendly chat. The attorney may praise your skill in investigation and lead you into boasting or a show of self-glorification that will leave a very bad impression on the jury. The "friendly" defense attorney may also try to lead you into testifying about evidence of which you have no personal knowledge. This error will be immediately exposed and your testimony tainted, if not completely discredited.

At the opposite extreme is the defense attorney who appears outraged by statements you make and goes on the attack immediately. This kind of attorney appears very excited and outraged, as though the trial is a travesty of justice. A natural reaction to such an approach is to exaggerate your testimony or lose your temper, which is exactly what the defense attorney wants. If you show anger, the jury may believe you are more interested in obtaining a conviction than determining the truth. It is often hard for a jury to believe that the well-dressed, meek-appearing defendant in court is the person who was armed with a gun and robbed a store. Maintain your dignity and impartiality, and show concern for only the facts.

The credibility of your testimony can be undermined in many ways. The defense may attempt to show that you are prejudiced, have poor character, or are interested only in seeing your arrest "stick." If asked, "Do you want to see the defendant convicted?" reply that you are there to present the facts you know and that you will abide by the court's decision. No contemporary case demonstrated these cross-examination attacks on police credibility more effectively than the O.J. Simpson murder trial. The defense was successful in shifting the focus away from the issue of the defendant's guilt and putting it directly on the incompetence of the police investigators.

The defense may also try to show that your testimony itself is erroneous because you are incompetent, lack information, are confused, have forgotten facts, or could not have had personal knowledge of the facts you have testified to. Do not respond to such criticism. Let your testimony speak for itself. If the defense criticizes your reference to notes, state that you simply want to be completely accurate. Be patient. If the defense counsel becomes excessively offensive, the prosecutor will intervene. Alternatively, the prosecutor may see that the defense is hurting its own case by such behavior and will allow the defense attorney to continue.

The defense attorney may further try to force contradictions or inconsistencies by incessantly repeating questions using slightly different wording. Repeat your previous answer. If the defense claims that your testimony does not agree with that of other officers, do not change your testimony. Whether your testimony is like theirs or different is irrelevant. The defense will attack it either way. If it is exactly alike, the defense will allege collusion. If it is slightly different, the defense will exaggerate this to convince the jury that the differences are so great that the officers are not even testifying about the same circumstances.

Rutledge (*Courtroom*, p. 77) explains that a favorite tactic of defense lawyers to destroy credibility is to try to get you to commit yourself to something and then later have to admit you could be wrong about it. He suggests that if either attorney asks for any kind of *measurement* you did not personally make, including distance, time, height, weight, speed, age, and the like, allow yourself some leeway. Either give an *approximation*—for example, "he was approximately 45 feet away"—or put your answer in brackets. **Brackets** provide a range—for example, "he was 40 to 50 feet away."

Another defense tactic is to use an accusatory tone in asking whether you talked with others about the case and what they told you about how to testify. Such accusations may make inexperienced officers feel guilty because they know they have talked about the case with many people. Because the accusing tone implies that this was legally incorrect, the officers may reply that they talked to no one. Such a response is a mistake because you may certainly discuss the case before testifying. Simply state that you have discussed the case with several people in an official capacity, but that none of them told you how to testify.

If defense counsel asks whether you have refreshed your memory before testifying, do not hesitate to say "yes." You would be a poor witness if you had not done so. Discussions with the prosecution, officers, and witnesses and a review of notes and reports are entirely proper. They assist you in telling the truth, the main purpose of testimony.

Leading questions are another defense tactic. For example, defense counsel may ask, "When did you first strike the defendant?" This implies that you did in fact strike the defendant. Defense attorneys also like to ask questions that presume that you have already testified to something when in fact you may not have done so. If you are misquoted, call it to the counsel's attention and then repeat the facts you testified to. If you do not remember your exact testimony, have it read from the court record.

In addition, defense counsel may ask complicated questions and then say, "Please answer 'yes' or 'no.'" Obviously, some questions cannot be answered that simply. Ask to have the question broken down. No rule requires a specific answer. If the court does not grant your request, answer the question as directed and let the prosecutor bring out the information through redirect examination.

Rapid-fire questioning is yet another tactic that defense attorneys use to provoke unconsidered answers. Do not let the attorney's pace rush you. Take time to consider your responses.

Do not be taken in by the "silent treatment." The defense attorney may remain silent for what seems like many seconds after you answer a question. If you have given a complete answer, wait patiently. Do *not* attempt to fill the silence by saying things such as, "At least that's how I remember it," or "It was something very close to that."

Another tactic frequently used by defense attorneys is to mispronounce officers' names intentionally or address them by the wrong rank. This is an attempt to distract the officer.

Regardless of how your testimony is attacked, treat the defense counsel as respectfully as you do the prosecutor. Do not regard the defense counsel as your enemy. You are in court to state the facts and tell the truth. Your testimony should exhibit no personal prejudice or animosity, and you should not become excited or provoked at defense counsel. Be professional.

Few officers are prepared for the rigor of testifying in court, even if they have received training in this area. Until officers have actually testified in court, they cannot understand how difficult it is. Because police officers are usually the primary and most damaging witnesses in a criminal case, defense attorneys know they must attempt to confuse, discredit, or destroy the officers' testimony.

The best testimony is accurate, truthful, and in accordance with the facts. Every word an officer says is recorded and may be played back or used by the defense. A key to testifying during cross-examination is to NEVER volunteer any information.

Garland and Stuckey (p. 515) explain that during cross-examination the defense attorney can ask questions about only subjects raised by the prosecution during direct examination. If an investigator volunteers additional information, he or she may open up areas the prosecution did not intend to present and may not be prepared for.

**Handling Objections**

Gardner and Anderson (p. 97) describe three categories of objections. The first category is objections to the *form of the question*: leading, speculative, argumentative, misstates facts in evidence, assumes facts not in evidence, vague and ambiguous, repetitive or cumulative, or misleading. The second category is objections to the *substance of the question*: irrelevant, immaterial, incompetent, calls for hearsay, insufficient foundation, calls for inadmissible opinion, or beyond the scope of the direct examination. The third category is objections to the *answer*: unresponsive, inadmissible opinion, inadmissible hearsay statement.

Rutledge (*Courtroom*, pp. 97-115) gives the following suggestions for handling objections:

> There are at least 44 standard trial objections in most states. We're only going to talk about the two that account for upwards of 90 percent of the problems a testifying officer will have: that your answer is a conclusion, or that it is nonresponsive.
>
> - How to avoid conclusions. One way is to listen to the form of the question. You know the attorney is asking you to speculate when he starts his questions with these loaded phrases:
>     Would you assume...?
>     Do you suppose...?
>     Don't you think that...?
>     Couldn't it be that...?
>     Do you imagine...?
>     Wouldn't it be fair to presume...?
>     Isn't it strange that...?
>     And the one you're likely to hear most often:
>     Isn't it possible that...?
> - Another major area of conclusionary testimony is what I call mindreading. You can't get inside someone else's brain. That means you don't know for a fact—so you can't testify—as to what someone else sees, hears, feels, thinks or wants and you don't know for a fact what somebody is trying to do, or is able to do, or whether he is nervous, excited, angry, scared, happy, upset, disturbed, or in any of the other emotional states that can only be labeled with a conclusion.
> - How to give "responsive" answers. You have to answer just the question you're asked—no more, no less. That means you have to pay attention to how the question is framed. You answer a yes-or-no question with a "yes" or "no."
>     Q: Did he perform the alphabet test?
>     A: Yes, twice—but he only went to "G."

Everything after the "yes" is nonresponsive. The officer anticipated the next three questions and volunteered the answers. He should have limited each answer to one question:

Q: Did he perform the alphabet test?
A: Yes.
Q: How many times?
A: Twice.
Q: How far did he go correctly the first time?
A: To the letter "G."

To avoid objections to your testimony, avoid conclusions and nonresponsive answers. Answer yes-or-no questions with "yes" or "no."

### Concluding Your Testimony

Do not leave the stand until instructed to do so by counsel or the court. As you leave the stand, do not pay special attention to the prosecution, defense counsel, defendant, or jury. Return immediately to your seat in the courtroom or leave the room if you have been sequestered. If you are told you may be needed for further testimony, remain available. If told you are no longer needed, leave the courtroom and resume your normal activities. To remain gives the impression that you have a special interest in the case.

If you are in the courtroom at the time of the verdict, show neither approval nor disapproval at the outcome. If you have been a credible witness and told the truth, win or lose in court, you have done your job and should not take the outcome personally.